Time Management

How to Awaken Your True Self and Reach Your Goals Fast With Enhanced Productivity

(How to Rewire Your Brain, Stop Addictions, Decluttering and Organizing Literally Everything)

Jeff LaPorte

Published by Kevin Dennis

© Jeff LaPorte

All Rights Reserved

Time Management: How to Awaken Your True Self and Reach Your Goals Fast With Enhanced Productivity (How to Rewire Your Brain, Stop Addictions, Decluttering and Organizing Literally Everything)

ISBN 978-1-989920-98-5

All rights reserved. No part of this guide may be reproduced in any form without permission in writing from the publisher except in the case of brief quotations embodied in critical articles or reviews.

Legal & Disclaimer

The information contained in this book is not designed to replace or take the place of any form of medicine or professional medical advice. The information in this book has been provided for educational and entertainment purposes only.

The information contained in this book has been compiled from sources deemed reliable, and it is accurate to the best of the Author's knowledge; however, the Author cannot guarantee its accuracy and validity and cannot be held liable for any errors or omissions. Changes are periodically made to this book. You must consult your doctor or get professional medical advice before using any of the suggested remedies, techniques, or information in this book.

Upon using the information contained in this book, you agree to hold harmless the Author from and against any damages, costs, and expenses, including any legal fees potentially resulting from the application of any of the information provided by this guide. This disclaimer applies to any damages or injury caused by the use and application, whether directly or indirectly, of any advice or information presented, whether for breach of contract, tort, negligence, personal injury, criminal intent, or under any other cause of action.

You agree to accept all risks of using the information presented inside this book. You need to consult a professional medical practitioner in order to ensure you are both able and healthy enough to participate in this program.

Table of Contents

INTRODUCTION 1

CHAPTER 1: STRESS AND STRESS MANAGEMENT DEFINED 8

CHAPTER 2: GETTING READY TO MEDITATE 13

CHAPTER 3: THE PSYCHOLOGY OF PROCRASTINATION.... 18

CHAPTER 4: GO STRONG, TAKE BREAKS........................... 21

CHAPTER 5: GROWING YOUR SKILL SET AND EMBRACING INNOVATION AND TECHNOLOGY 23

CHAPTER 6: CREATE YOUR TO-DO LIST 29

CHAPTER 7: IMPROVE YOUR TOLERANCE FOR DISCOMFORT 35

CHAPTER 8: ACTION – PRODUCTIVITY APPLIED 40

CHAPTER 9: BALANCE YOUR WORK LIFE/PERSONAL LIFE 46

CHAPTER 10: CHANGE HABITS THAT DISRUPT YOUR FOCUS IN 5 SIMPLE WAYS.. 51

CHAPTER 11: SEVEN AND EIGHT, YOU'RE DOING GREAT. 65

CHAPTER 12: MORNING RITUALS FOR HAPPINESS AND SATISFACTION 70

CHAPTER 13: EXTRA HABITS TO MAKE YOUR MORNING ROUTINE EVEN PEPPIER 78

CHAPTER 14: SET UP A STREAMLINED WORKSPACE 86

CHAPTER 15: HOW TO ORGANIZE YOUR PRIORITIES 90

CHAPTER 16: ORGANIZING YOURSELF AND YOUR MIND. 98

CHAPTER 17. FINDING INSPIRATION.............................. 107

CHAPTER 18: 5 LITTLE GOLDEN NUGGETS...................... 113

CHAPTER 19: BECOMING A PROCRASTINATION STRATEGIST.. 119

CHAPTER 20: BEING A MORE PRODUCTIVE STUDENT.... 126

CHAPTER 21: THE COMFORT ZONE FEAR OF SEPARATION AND FEAR OF INTIMACY.. 137

CHAPTER 22: ELIMINATING PROCRASTINATION............ 143

CHAPTER 23: DISCIPLINE YOUR REWARDS..................... 153

CHAPTER 24: VIEW THINGS FROM DIFFERENT PERSPECTIVES 158

CHAPTER 25: TAKE A NAP... 161

CHAPTER 26: BATHROOM HACKS................................... 164

CHAPTER 27: HABITS RELATED TO WEALTH AND PRODUCTIVITY 170

CHAPTER 28: UPGRADE YOUR KEY SKILLS...................... 178

CHAPTER 29: RULES TO GET YOU STARTED WITH YOUR TO-DO LIST... 182

CHAPTER 30: REFRAMING FAILURE FAILURE AND PROCRASTINATION 186

CONCLUSION.. 191

Introduction

*Have you ever felt fear to start a whole new thing in your life? Are you slow to pursue either studies or a new career because you think it will not work out? Or you are exhausted of been just an employee at some company, but you have to keep on working there because you fear if you quit and go start your own business it won't work?

*Fear is the reason why most people are afraid of taking risks. This feeling is among the very strongest feelings a human can have or experience. People reluctantly get into new activities with the perception of the worst yet they don't focus on the positive results of the action.

*Different people have different perceptions of life, and with such a diversity some people then take advantage of the fear in them and make a good fortune from it.

*Fear as many people perceive it, think it always works against us, but no, that is not always the case. Even the most successful people in different areas have their fears but they don't accept it overcome them. Fear is an inevitable feeling what makes the difference between us is how to handle this feeling.

*Now here we are going to look at how fear is an asset and how to make a fortune from it. Fear exposes one to new experiences which you never knew or expected to do. For you to overcome fear, then you must do that which you fear.

*An example of this is if you are afraid and want to do public speaking then you will have to learn good public speaking skills by having an audience .No matter how small the audience will be, you will definitely not be good at once but as you go up the ladder, then you will have to do frequent public speaking sessions with you as the speaker or as part of the audience.

*Other fears are those of other people's opinion and public approval. An example of this is if someone is eating irresponsible and losing fitness daily. An example is for the public people who are always on television especially in the show biz. They have to exercise daily, hit the gym well which is not only helping them in public but, also helping their bodies.

*In a case of an invention one is fearful of starting or introducing a new product into the market. This then results to delayed activities, but also the same person is afraid of been broke, so they are left with no other choice but to sell or market their products

*Fear helps one act instantly and address issues as they come since one gets afraid of the future results. Fear makes you look at the long-term effect of postponing a particular activity. If a company has continuous decrease in its sales then from the fear of collapsing in the future the management deals with the situation instantly.

*Focus then is also brought up by fear of failure. One gets a sense of direction and pursues that course to the very end to prevent or escape from failure which is a

fear of very many if not all companies and entrepreneurs.

*Fear sometimes is an indicator that something is wrong or things are moving in the wrong direction. This indication is often a fact but not always the truth. If one is fearful of something, then they are not confident enough of what they are doing even if it is right.

*Fear creeps in inform of discouragement, and demoralization follows. A good example of this fact is that if you are growing huge and not proportionate daily, you get the fear of other people's opinion and more so the diseases that you get exposed to. This is an indication that something is not right and you are not headed in the right direction. For you to mitigate this situation, then you start hitting the gym and eating healthy diets.

*Fear comes hand in hand with courage. Most people think or believe that the successful people in the world have no fears or concerns, but that is not a good perception for these people experienced fear but they gained courage to face these fears.

* If one conquers something, then they gain much courage to continue. Fear then is necessary since it increases courage and propels one to new greater heights.

*Fear also helps us identify what is more important to us. If you get a lot of setbacks in life at once like, having a sick kid, your business is recording losses, your marriage is falling apart, and you are disagreements with your parents, then since you can't solve all these issues at a go, one has to prioritize these things in their weight of importance.

*The fear of crumbling down of your life with the fear of losing you loved ones then makes you prioritize things and sought them fast.

*Fear also has quite some health benefits by raising your immune system. A research of people taken to a movie theater and watched a horror movie shows that physiological fear responses caused the movie watchers to experience a lift of inactivated white blood cells, keeping them from viral infections.

*Fear is not a feeling for specific people, but it is a feeling felt by anyone and everyone at different stages of the human life. How we deal with this feeling is different to different people. Not everything that is seen good gets cute quotes, fear too has its couple of quotes saying how important it is in the human life.

*Some of the quotes include;

"fear is nothing much than an obstacle that stands in the way of progress and success"

"by overcoming our fear we come out stronger and wiser within ourselves."

"Take every chance and drop every fear."

"Sometimes change can be scary, but you know what's scarier? Allowing fear to stop you from growing, evolving and progressing."

"Let fear not shake you or stop from pursuing your dream because if you get scared, delay or stop, someone else out there will defeat the fear and you will be out shined."

Chapter 1: Stress And Stress Management Defined

We all have experienced stress in our lives and it would not be wrong to say that it is something natural for humans. The problem is what we do to keep stress away from hampering our daily lives. Stress Management is probably one of the most researched subjects of the world. A lot has been established about this subject and a lot is still to be discovered.

The accepted and settled theories about stress management and a common man belief have often been in a state of warfare. This is exactly where it gets a little hard to define stress management. Even if we talk about modern science, there are many research and reports that differ a great deal from each other. I have tried to express and define this subject from a common man's perspective. Without being too philosophical about it, here is what I have come up with….

Stress is a state (usually associated with mental health) of a human being, which often relates to how an individual reacts to a challenge, unexpected or a tough situation or environment. Stress is usually considered negative for humans as this could result into some serious physical or mental problems if not dealt with accordingly.

However, there are some unique people who tend to perform at their best only if they are exposed to stress. This may be referred to as positive stress, which brings the best out of us without posing any threat or danger to our physical or mental health. Positive stress is extremely rare and lacks proper scientific establishments as well.

This definition of stress by Richard R. Lzarus is straight from the text books and is commonly accepted by physicians,

"Stress is a condition or feeling experienced when a person perceives that demands exceed the personal and social resources that the individual is able to mobilize"

A helpful and beneficial way of dealing with stress and not letting it buildup is known as stress management. It can be more clearly defined as a method to control stress with the help of diversified and proven techniques. These techniques may also be in the shape of physical exercise like "physiotherapies".

Stress if allowed to go untreated may start showing symptoms of depression, which is chiefly responsible for a sharp decline in physical and mental health. Through various techniques of stress management, a depressed human being can lead a happy and joyous life.

It is not easy as life can be real tough at times, we have to go through situations that are tailor-made to bring anxiety and depression. Stress management techniques are ideal in this situation to manage all the negativity and transform our lives into a more pleasurable experience.

Our work place is the favorite breeding ground for Stress. According to a recent research which focused on average business professional in United States concluded that following are the main reasons for unsustainable stress at work place:

1- Too many projects at one time

2- Interruptions and distractions from work (according to this study this amounts to 2.5 hours a day)

3- Downsizing

4- Politics within office

5- And many more...

These may be the reasons why some of the adults go through sleepless nights, thinking of the cumbersome day and challenges ahead. Stress in this case is inevitable but we can adapt a lifestyle and learn techniques that can help us fight against stress.

The rest of this e-book will be focusing on various techniques to overcome stress at work and some of the tips that could really help us stay on top of our daily tasks.

Chapter 2: Getting Ready To Meditate

Find a quiet spot, sitting comfortably with eyes closed and meditating looks very easy if you go by its face value. But meditation is definitely not a cake walk. Beginners find it tough and often frustrating when they start meditating and do not achieve what they are looking for.

The process of meditation is tremendously relative. How you feel after a meditative session greatly depends on your preparation and mindset. Your mind is an assortment of your experiences. When you experience something, you tend to respond to the situation. However, while meditating, you are supposed to let thoughts flow in and out without responding. It is all about participatory observation. This is very tricky as your mind is like a river and if not directed will keep wandering around. Thus, before you begin meditation you need to prepare yourself for it.

Don't Set Expectations: Whenever you invest your time in anything new, you tend to expect something out of it. However, you must teach yourself to relax and let meditation work for you in its own way. Be open to it. Store away all your preconceptions, ideas, and expectations as they will come in your way while meditating. Sit back and patiently observe. What emerges out of your meditation may or may not match with your expectations. That's ok!

Be Patient with Yourself: Meditation is about silent contemplation, not about aggression. Try to be patient, stress-free and stable while you meditate. If you think you need time to get yourself into the meditative state, take a break. Start when you are ready. There is not time limit for meditation. When you start, you might be uncomfortable sitting for more than 10 minutes. If that is the case, stop and wait till you feel ready for it.

Take your own time: Settle yourself in a comfortable and quiet place and take your time. Be patient with yourself. The idea is to relax so don't induce stress and don't rush.

Keep an Open and Positive Mind: While you close your eyes, thoughts and experience will float in an out. Let them flow but don't cling on to them for long. Keep yourself open to good and bad experiences and try to get comfortable in their presence. Don't regret or blame yourself for anything. Don't run from your problems or bear them in saintly silence. Recognize them and look upon them as opportunities to learn and grow.

Don't look for Solutions Right away: Meditation is not your 'problem-solver'. Definitely not at this stage when you are just a beginner. So don't expect magical solutions to emerge for your current issues. Don't try to reason out things. Just approach them with wordless bare attention.

Choose a Suitable Time: Meditation aims at relaxing your mind and body. So don't strain yourself to meditate when you know you have a train to take in the next

30 minutes. Choose a convenient time when you know you do not have any appointments or are not likely to be disturbed by a guest. Early mornings and bedtime are the best time to consider meditation.

Find a Quiet Place: Meditation requires solitude. You surely cannot meditate while your kids are playing with their Legos and Blocks. A quiet and peaceful place is a definite pre-requisite for a successful meditation.

Check out Your Posture: Meditation can be done in the posture you are most comfortable in. You can sit up straight with an erect spine and relaxed shoulders. You can also try lying down, but be sure not to doze off. The Padmasana (the lotus position) is the widely preferred posture for meditation.

Neither Binge on Food nor Starve yourself before Meditating: Binging on food can make you feel sleepy while meditating and you will miss the plot. On the other hand not having any food might force you to constantly think of food while meditating. So be sure to have a light meal at least an hour prior to your meditation.

10. Open Your Eyes Gently once you Finish: Don't be in a hurry to end your meditative state. The entire idea is to feel calm and relaxed. Hence, don't be in a hurry to open your eyes and get on to your work. Instead, slowly open your eyes, rub your palms against each other and feel you face with them slowly and gently.

Chapter 3: The Psychology Of Procrastination

The biggest problem we face is that procrastination is an easy thing to do. Our brain loves easy, and choosing the easiest path to perceived success helps activate those portions which make us happy. Generally, we all tend to do tasks that make us feel good now but put off harder or unpleasant ones to finish later. The simple reason behind this is that we love success, and any task that has doubt about its success may mean failure, so we avoid it just in case we may fail.

There's also a genuine fear of success for some people. Success often means change, and if you're successful then there will be questions about "what next." We put things off because we worry about what happens after and whether the "after" we're chasing will end up being a failure that releases those nasty pain chemicals into the brain. You worry, therefore you put it off until you are confident and that may never happen.

Perfectionism can also lead to procrastination. The desire to see the goal through to a high standard, while admirable, often gives us perfect opportunity to claim that we're not finished yet. Perfectionism can be practical if it makes the task complete, but when it causes anxiety and neurotics, it leads to procrastination. This type of procrastination is like a few of flying for someone who "wants to travel," the fear of actually succeeding means trying so by putting the task off you don't have to try.

The Procrastinating Brain

Sometimes we forget things. In the first part of this book, I mentioned that the brain transfers unpleasant tasks into short-term memory so that they can be casually forgotten. Here's where we can start fixing this improving our cognition. The Hippocampus is responsible for forming memories, and rather than working on autopilot and hoping we remember the task actively improving your memory can stop you using forgetfulness as a procrastination tool.

The easiest way to improve cognition is to be active. Activities that require focus and participation are especially useful. You can also choose activities that you find challenging or that make you think. Memories are nothing more than electrical pathways in the brain so the more you use those pathways, the more familiar you are, kinda like your route home each day.

Stress can also lead to poor cognition because it releases any number of disruptive hormones and chemicals. So while you might be stressed because you procrastinate, you could also be procrastinating because of your stress. Consider stress relief methods like yoga, meditation, or even just getting more sleep to calm those raging chemicals and think clearer.

Chapter 4: Go Strong, Take Breaks

The people who have trouble with procrastination in their everyday life have this vision of the other half; they think that people who come off as "productive" work effortlessly for hours and hours at a time. They think it's an easy thing to do for some while they simply fail to have the luck of possessing that skill.

The truth is that even very prolific people need to take breaks. Very few people work without stop for hours and hours. Firstly, a person would lose their mind if they did that. A modicum of sanity needs to be retained. If you make your work-time that miserable you will never want to work; thus, you will dread that time and put if off even more. The brain cannot take eight hours of intense mental strain with no stoppage.

There is another very important reason why you need to take breaks throughout the process: if you don't, the work will suffer. The entire purpose of implementing a system to get rid of procrastination and increase productivity is to produce good work. Put it this way: would you rather have a twenty-five minute presentation that's total nonsense or a very solid ten-minute presentation? Working nonstop is more likely to produce a high volume of bad work. The goal is to produce good work at a reasonable rate. Don't work yourself to death.

So how, practically speaking, does this break system work? What I like to do is sit down at my workstation and begin work. I tell myself that I need to complete one aspect of the project to its completion and then I can stop. So I work hard for an hour or two and then I stand up and stretch or get a snack. I then go right back to work and work another section. In this way, I don't ever feel overwhelmed or burnt out. The short breaks rejuvenate me and recharge my brain a little bit. You are more likely to get things done in this way than to work than work yourself towards the precipice of exhaustion.

Chapter 5: Growing Your Skill Set And Embracing Innovation And Technology

Tip Three: Grow your Skill Set

"Education is the catalyst that will hone and sharpen our skills and abilities and cause them to blossom."

-Joseph B. Wirthlin

After you have worked for a long time it is very easy to fall into certain patterns where you never change your way of doing things. In today's world, however, trends change every second literally, and this is in each and every industry. As a result, it is very easy to find yourself stuck to old ways of working that are no longer relevant or productive for your industry. What is the solution for this then? The solution in this case therefore is to invest in your skills. If you have only a bachelors,' go on to get your degree. There are also industry based trainings and conferences where you can learn more on the newest skills and trends in your industry.

You can also learn from fellow employees since each of you possess a special set of skills. In today's world with the multitudes of online short courses available, you should challenge yourself to take at least two or three short courses every month. This will greatly build your mental capacity and equip you with multiple skills. Online sources like Coursera and Alison among many others offer short courses designed by some of the best universities from across the world. The good news is that a good number of the courses are actually free of charge!

The best way to track this is to set goals such as done above. Another one can be to attend at least one big conference every quarter. This puts you in a position to network and mingle with people in your industry, understand what they are doing and compare it to what you are doing! In the end, there still remains so much to be learned and this will be covered in more detail under the technology sector.

Tip Four: Embrace Innovation and Use of Technology

"Learning and innovation go hand in hand. The ignorance of success is to think that what you did yesterday will be sufficient for tomorrow."

- William Pollard

This is best explained in a simple example. Take two workers who have to compile data from two separate sheets. One has vast knowledge of different kinds of files while another one only knows how to use their calculator probably. With a simple input for example on an excel sheet, the values can be summed up to give a total value and include any other variations required for example finding the difference between two or more values and so on. So between these two people, who is more likely to finish this task faster and move on to other things?

We are currently living in probably one of the most technologically developed times throughout humanity. This simply means that for everything you are doing, there is most likely someone who has developed a way to do it faster and better. Therefore, this means that there is a sure way to always ensure that you are as productive as is humanly possible and that you use as little time as possible on each task. Benefits of employing technology to ensure maximum productivity include:

Reduced overall time per task. Use of the right programs and technology in general can reduce the amount of time you spend on a task by more than half when done right. This means that in the time you would take to do a single task you could now easily do two! If that doesn't spell productivity, I do not know what does!

Minimal likelihood for human error. The beauty of technology is that if you make any error, the computer will detect it almost instantly! This reduces on time spent struggling to find a single error, and it makes your work more accurate.

Enhances mobility. In most cases, employing technology into your work helps you to become more mobile, giving you the ability to do your work remotely from anywhere you are. Carrying some work home no longer means walking with a pile of files.

Increased efficiency and effectiveness. Productivity is synonymous with efficiency. It is only when you learn to be effective and efficient in your work that you will attain maximum productivity. Technology is an easy and sure way to get started on this.

There is a bevy of apps and programs to choose from whichever industry you are in. Moreover, platforms like YouTube have made learning or mastery of new technology at 3 minute affair. Remember, the hardest part is always taking the first step. The learning curve that follows is simply a smooth procession going forward. Last but not least, remember that the Internet is your friend! Whatever information you may need however complex, there is a 99% chance that the solution can be found online. Get using technology and innovation to your advantage!

Chapter 6: Create Your To-Do List

The things you do each day can help you achieve your goals or they can hinder your progress if you allow them to. This is why you need to create a to-do list. This is a list that shows all the activities you engage in during a particular day. A to-do list helps you see which activities occupy your time. It gives you greater control of your time and enables you to shift your focus to important things.

Another important thing a to-do list helps you to do is avoid procrastination. How so? Well, this has to do with the type of tasks you will have on your to-do list. Your to-do list should be categorized into various types of tasks. These include tasks that are:

Important

The first thing you need to determine is which tasks are important. Important tasks are usually the ones that contribute the most value to your life. That is, when you do then, you get a lot in return. But when you don't do them, you have a lot to lose.

For example, completing a school project adds on to your grade. Thus, the project becomes important because it is of high value. If you don't complete it, it may lead to a failing grade.

It's also good to note that important tasks often affect other people or other projects. If you don't do them, something else or someone else may end up suffering. For example, if you work at a factory and your electricity bill is due, you need to pay it first. This is because your machines won't be able to run if the power is cut off. Tasks that have to be completed first, because other tasks depend on them are important tasks.

Urgent

Urgent tasks are the type of tasks that need your immediate attention. If you don't do such tasks, you'll face immediate consequences. Urgent tasks can be high value tasks or low value tasks. For example, a high value project that is due soon qualifies as an urgent task. On the other hand, taking out your trash during 'trash day' can qualify as a low value task but both of these tasks are urgent.

It is also important to note that the sense of urgency is affected by deadlines. For example, completing a project is important but it only becomes urgent if the due date is close by. If you have a month to complete the project, that takes the urgency away as you can easily work through it a little at a time. But if you leave the project until the last day, then the sense of urgency increases greatly. In other words, just because a task is important it doesn't mean that it is urgent.

Not Urgent

Some tasks are not urgent. They don't require your immediate attention. They may be important but you can do them at a later time. But as you've seen, the sense of urgency can be influenced by time. Thus, tasks that fall in this category may vary depending on your deadline. If you decide to do a task at the last minute, it becomes urgent. Thus, plan your time wisely.

Not important

Some tasks are simply not important but you may love doing them. Many of such tasks are low value tasks. They won't bring you much gain and you can live without them. For example, browsing the internet in search of something to watch is not important but you may end up devoting a lot of your time to that task.

Once you've written down all your tasks, you need to group them further into:

Urgent and important tasks – These are tasks that should take priority on your to-do list. You should make it a point to handle them first before you attempt any other tasks. Once you are through with the list, you can move on to the next category.

Important but not urgent tasks – Such tasks need your attention but they don't have to be done right now. However, it would be wise to determine when you're going to do them. This way, you can pace yourself and complete them without being in a rush.

Urgent but not important tasks – You can actually delegate these tasks to other people. They need not consume your time if you can help it.

Not important and not urgent tasks – These are tasks that should not consume your time.

It takes self-discipline to complete your tasks. A to-do list enhances your self-discipline. It gives you a clear path to follow and shows you what you need to do at any given time.

Make it a habit to tackle all your priority tasks first. These tasks are urgent and important and they are often the hardest to accomplish. Once you complete them, you'll have an easier time going about your day simply because you've gotten them out of the way.

Many people find it helpful to create a to-do list before they sleep at night. This habit is advantageous in that it helps you to plan for the next day. This way, when you wake up, you already know what you need to do. You will not spend a lot of time trying to figure out what you need to do first. It would also help to prepare your things for the next day.

Remember, your habits will affect your self-discipline. Developing good habits equips you for success. You can prepare for the next day by selecting the clothes you will wear, brushing your shoes and packing your bag. Also, ensure that your keys and any other thing you might need are within reach.

The idea is to give yourself the best chance to start your day right. This will set the tone for the rest of your day. Once you get up, you can start working on your to-do list. Of course, if you're not used to following a to-do list, you'll face some challenges. But you can overcome them by improving your tolerance to discomfort.

Chapter 7: Improve Your Tolerance For Discomfort

Self-control is one of the aspects of self-discipline. It fuels self-discipline, and provides checks and balances such that you can easily tell when you lose control. When you lose control, you give into your bad habits and allow procrastination to throw you off your path.

Unfortunately, it is easy to lose self-control if you have low tolerance for discomfort. Think about it. It is easy to do something you love doing because it 'comes naturally'. You do not have to try very hard to accomplish it because it gives you pleasure.

On the other hand, you may find it difficult to do something you don't like even if it is a simple task. This is because such activities bring you a measure of discomfort. You're doing them because you have to not because you want to. You would rather do something else in their place.

But here's the thing.

You cannot achieve your goals by ignoring tasks that bring you discomfort. It doesn't work that way. This is why you need to increase your tolerance for discomfort. You can do this if you:

Accept Frustration

Frustration is part of life but how you react to it can make all the difference as to whether you will fail or succeed at accomplishing your goals.

If you allow frustration to take the center stage in your day to day life, you'll find yourself looking for ways to avoid tasks that frustrate you. However, if you learn to live with frustration, you won't feel the need to give up on a task just because you're a little frustrated. Rather, you will soldier on because the frustration has been relegated to a small part of your life.

If you're doing a task and you reach a hurdle, don't assume that you can't overcome it. Instead, take a step back, look at the situation objectively and then write down the steps you'll take to tackle the task. This way, you will learn that frustration is a temporary feeling. Once you work to solve the problem, you are left with a feeling of accomplishment.

Change Your Perspective

You need to change your perspective if you want to have an easier time tolerating discomfort. Think about it. The discomfort you feel from having to complete your tasks is nothing compared to the discomfort you will feel if you end up not doing them.

If you start procrastinating and postponing your tasks, you'll soon find yourself suffering from things such as anxiety because you 'waited too long' before making the necessary changes.

Don't let temporary discomfort cloud your vision. If you plan your day well, you will have enough time to complete your tasks and still indulge in your wants. Thus, instead of looking for ways to avoid uncomfortable tasks, you should be looking for ways to do them fast and effectively so that you can move on to tasks that actually bring you pleasure.

Also, keep in mind that while some tasks are difficult to do, they will bring you great results in future. Do not lose sight of that. If you keep that in mind, you will be better at exercising self-control and sticking to your tasks.

Practice Patience

In life, you're faced with situations that call for patience. For example, you may be waiting for someone, waiting for a call, waiting to be served, waiting for the bus and so forth.

Such situations can teach you to be patient. You can use that time constructively instead of becoming impatient. For example, if you're waiting for a call, instead of checking your phone every few seconds, you can decide to listen to an audio book or finish up your chores. The idea is to shift your mind to what you're doing at present instead of focusing on what you want to do at a later time.

When you fill your time with something constructive, you won't feel like you're wasting it. It becomes time well spent. Patience teaches you that there are some things worth waiting for. It helps improve your self-control and self-discipline. Thus, you will be better able to stick to what you start because you are no longer used to instant gratification.

Overall, it is always important to remember that self control is something that you can build if you work on it. If you learn to live with frustration, change your perspective and practice patience, you'll be able to increase your tolerance for discomfort and this will allow you to control your reactions. Apart from tolerating discomfort, there is something else that can enhance your self-control and self-discipline. This is mental toughness. Let's see how you can increase your mental toughness.

Chapter 8: Action – Productivity Applied

You have changed your mindset and are still determined that getting rid of procrastination episodes is just the right thing to do. You are getting closer to being maximally productive with overcome laziness with each hack you master and with each advice you accept. Now when you have arranged your tasks, made a list and arranged your surroundings, it is time to apply all that on working on tasks from your list, one task at the time. We will present you with hacks that will help you with completing your tasks painlessly and promptly.

Hack #16: Proper handling of To-do-lists

You have already made your list the night before D day. You will be doing that for each next day to make it easier to follow up with all the things you need to do. Even if there are only a couple of things you need to take care of, still make a list. Crossing everything you did from the list will make you feel the sense of achievement, which is a great feeling. We have showed you how to make a list and stressed out its importance, but you will now learn how to take care of those lists. Now, with making to-do lists, you always need to put the hardest thing to be done first, going down with easier tasks. The easiest task should be done the last even though many people leave the hardest for the end that never happens as you procrastinate. Leaving hard tasks to be done the last will only encourage your procrastination as you will that way avoid finishing that hard task. So, hard tasks to the top, easy tasks take the bottom of the list. Each task should have estimated time of completion and each task should have a 15 minute break if it lasts for more than 2-3 hours to finish it. Also include bigger breaks in your to-do list when you have many tasks to complete.

Hack #17: Follow up

This is very important to keep you on the track of productivity. Whatever you do, do not cheat on your to-do list. You can't allow yourself to change break times and/or make breaks longer, doing something that is not on your list. That would be procrastinating. Always follow up with the timeline you have made for your list as you have yourself made it to match your responsibilities for that day. There is enough time for everything.

Hack #18: Don't think about hours

It often happens when you finally sit to work on your task, that you start thinking for how long you will be working on it, being stuck on predicting how boring or exhausting it will be while you are working on it. That might be a trigger that will make you give up and get back to doing nothing. Instead of thinking about how long it will take you to complete your task, start working on it with being focused solely on the task. You can set your alarm clock to remind you when it's the break time so you would let your mind at ease and quit thinking about time. That way you will be able to focus on your work.

Hack #19: Break the tasks

If you are stuck with a large task that will take you hours to do, don't leave it for the last minute when you will be stressing out under pressure of finishing it as fast as you can. Instead, break that large task into smaller tasks, making it easier to complete. You will make an outline for completing it, planning the entire task, then if you have a deadline of couple of days, you will divide it into smaller tasks and work on it every day as planned by then outline. That way, the big task won't look so big and won't intimidate you, giving you excuses not to work and be productive.

Hack #20: 15 minute rule

If you are having troubles getting focused on having your assignments done whenever you have to sit and work on something for more than an hour, you can try with the 25 minute rule. If you still can't handle long periods of productivity, you can try taking a 5 minute break on every 15 minutes. You will use those five minutes to check your phone, stretch your legs or just relax. Then, you will get back to work for another round of 15 minutes and so on until you are done with the task. If you are the most productive in short time spans with breaks then you should definitely try with 15 minute rule and see if it's working for you.

Hack #21: No Smart phone allowed

Smart phones are major distractions and will surely keep you busy in vain, messing with your productivity in all negative ways possible. Someone will message you and you will reply, you will get caught up with chatting with someone, you might even start playing Candy Crash Saga, update your Facebook status and follow up with likes, scroll down the news feed on every social network you have account on, and so on. Our advice is to keep your smart phone away from your workspace while you are working. You are allowed to take a look at it or reply only if there is an emergency call or during your breaks. That will motivate you into being more productive instead of having your smart phone help you with procrastinating.

Chapter 9: Balance Your Work Life/Personal Life

"Somehow, we'll find it. The balance between whom we wish to be and whom we need to be. But for now, we simply have to be satisfied with who we are." – Brandon Sanderson

When Jack went to work every day, he came home with all of his work ideas still going on in his head. He paid very little attention to his family or his persona life and appeared to be living for work. When I pointed this out, it appeared that he didn't believe that he could balance out work life and home life, so I introduced the habits in the last chapter and this helped him to free up time for his family. It's important that you do. If you give everything that you are to your work, your home life suffers. If you are always talking about your family at work, your work life suffers. You need to strike a good balance and the best balance of all is to only think of work while you are there. Let's face it, no matter how you believe yourself to be irreplaceable, you are not. If you drop dead tomorrow, someone else will be taken on to do your job. However, if you drop dead tomorrow, your family will be the biggest losers because they lose someone they happen to love. They chose you because of that love and you really do need to understand that sharing life isn't about abandoning your family for the sake of work each day and giving little in return.

Habit No. 10 – Apply the Pareto Principle

This is a very important principle that was invented by an Italian Architect. What he noticed was that 80 percent of the population of a certain Italian town worked for the financial benefit of 20 percent. That doesn't sound very fair, but it can be applied in all areas of your life. You put in 80 percent effort and get back 20 percent satisfaction in most area of your life. Thus, you need to swing the balance a little in your favor. When I approach this subject with clients, I draw a pair of scales.

This only needs to be very simple, but draw it onto a page and make it big enough to add all of the bad things on one side and all of the good things on the other. The chances are that your life is weighed against you and that the Pareto principle applies. The kind of things that you put on the negative side will be Bills to pay, work to do, bad things in your life. On the other side you put all the things in your life that make you happy. The idea of this exercise is to gradually increase the amount you have on the happy side of the scales so that you begin to see happiness in your life.

You also need to decrease the things on the negative side so that you end up with an equation that shows that you have more to be happy with than that which makes you miserable. For example, if your salary doesn't cover your outgoings, simplify your life so that it does. Who needs cable TV? Who needs all of these extra bills? Work out ways that you can make the negative side negligible and the wealth it gives you is truly something that you feel in your heart. The kind of things that can go on the positive side are things like:

Watch my child take his first steps

Enjoy an afternoon at the zoo with the kids.

Go out on a date night with my partner

Give myself a night out once a week

What you are doing is recognizing what you are doing with your life and you can add and subtract from either side of the scale by making small adjustments to your life. In one case, a client made the scales and had little stick on post-it notes that she used to show the positives and the negatives. She was so good at it by the time she had played around with all the elements of her life that she became an expert in balancing out her lifestyle. In fact, the last time that I visited her, she was starting her own business at home and thoroughly looking forward to it. She put this down to two things. One was prioritizing and the other was working on all the negative areas of her life. She had never seen the Pareto rule before and when she applied that to her life, she was able to balance her life in such a way that it made her a very happy person indeed and changed a lot of her priorities.

You can do the same thing too and it will show you where all your negative energies are coming from and what you can do to replace them. If that means saying "no" to overtime this week, then so be it. At least you won't miss your daughter's attempt at becoming a ballerina and she will go through her life remembering that you took time out of your busy schedule to include her! That's very important indeed. Absent parents miss so much of their children's growing up years and keeping enough energy for your life is vital to your enjoyment of it.

Chapter 10: Change Habits That Disrupt Your Focus In 5 Simple Ways

According to Zig Ziglar, a famous American motivational speaker, superstar salesperson, and author "Lack of direction, not lack of time is the problem. We all have twenty four-hour days."

Mr. Ziglar is 100% percent right: A lack of direction is why many of us cannot fulfill our genuine desires, move towards our goals, and increase our productivity. A lack of direction comes from a lack of focus and if you fix the habits that contribute to poor focus, you will successfully develop killer focus and in turn gain a sense of direction. A sense of direction shall help you manifest your desires. If you cannot focus on the important tasks, you will constantly jump from one task to the other in a never-ending cycle.

To help you rectify this, here are 4 behaviors guaranteed to help you change all the habits that destroy your focus so you can concentrate on what is important.

6: Stop Multitasking

One thing you need to remember is that just because you are capable of multi-tasking does not mean you should do it, as if you stop multitasking, you will be more productive.

Your brain can do wonders; no one is questioning your intelligence. However, why would you want to do five things at a time and not give your best to any of it? Would it not be wiser to do one thing at a time and be an absolute pro at it? The choice is yours.

The problem with multi-tasking is that you are using too much energy concentrating simultaneously on various things and therefore, it takes longer than usual to complete tasks you could have finished fast.

The best choice therefore, is to give complete attention to one task at a time and only move on to the next one when complete one task. This is going to make you much more productive and you will appreciate the results you shall see. Actually, when you stop multitasking, you shall start enjoying tasks as you complete them.

To stop multi-tasking, build the habit of completing one task at a time. If you have to create a report, concentrate on the report and nothing but the report and if your mind forces you to jump to another task or do 2 more tasks at the same time, remind yourself of what you are doing and why you are doing it.

Bring all your attention back to the task and pay full attention to each word as you write it. This helps you get more involved in the task and concentrate on it only. Do this with everything you do be it completing significant tasks or trivial ones. Doing this shall help you form the habit of completing one task at a time, which shall increase your productivity.

7: Prioritize Your Tasks

Your focus shifts from important tasks to insignificant ones because you fail to prioritize the former. An inability to prioritize your tasks and differentiate between important tasks that help boost productivity and those that lower your productivity or do not influence it majorly often makes you unproductive and inefficient.

If you start prioritizing your work, you will easily change your habit of focusing on lesser important tasks that do not help you fulfill your goals. As you begin to understand the chores that need your utmost attention and time, you start to prioritize them over the insignificant tasks. Naturally, when your focus shifts from what is trivial to what is important, you work on important tasks first; this increases your productivity.

To enjoy these amazing results, get into the habit of listing all your tasks for a week or a month beforehand and then segregate the ones that hardly influence your productivity whether it is work/professional productivity or that relate to personal and household chores.

Next, create a schedule to work on your important tasks first and use the hacks mentioned in the previous chapter to complete the high priority tasks on time.

8: Create a Positive and Conducive Work Environment

The inability to focus on your work is often a product of a cluttered, messy, and a negative workplace environment not conducive to work. To change your habit of not focusing on important tasks, you need to make some positive changes to your work environment.

Take a good look at your work environment and determine if you like sitting and working in it. If it is messy, full of clutter, unorganized and dull, you are likely to want to do something other than focus on your work.

A positive, clean, decluttered, organized and neat environment is conducive to work and helps you develop killer focus because in such an environment, you are around things that inspire and encourage you to work on important things. To build that environment, remove everything you no longer use from your workspace; do the same with everything else that does not add meaning or value to you.

If you have documents that relate to old projects you do not need any more, or documents you already have digital copies of, throw them away. If you own 5 staplers but only one works, toss the useless 4 in the bin and keep only one.

Moreover, clean your workspace of any dust, dirt, and rubbish and organize everything. Keep things in the colors blue and red in your office as blue improves your focus and red increases your energy and productivity. Try this technique once and you will stick to it forever because it will help you manage your inability to focus on your work.

9: Manage Your Distractions

How often do you work in absolute harmony and quiet? How often do you block out all your distractions first and work for 2 or more consecutive hours so you finish a certain task on time and can have lots of free time at your disposal? If you have an exceedingly low productivity, the answer is likely to be 'not so often'

Distractions are all the things that disrupt your focus, sidetrack you from your work, and engage you in unnecessary, extra, and meaningless activities. Chatting with a friend instead of cleaning your yard, watching movies on Netflix when you should be preparing a presentation due in 3 days, and napping for 2 hours instead of 1 when you knew you should visit the market and conduct a quick survey to improve your product are a few apt examples of distractions that lower your productivity.

To build a life where you accomplish all your goals and steadily move towards the success you envision, you have to become an effective distractions manager. To become one, start by identifying the distractions that distract you whenever you sit down to work. Make a note of all those disruptions and then find easy and effective ways to manage them.

If you have an urge to use Facebook as you work, switch off your phone or block access to the site for some time. If you have an in-home office and your children disturb you during work hours, you could work when they are at school or put them in daycare for a few hours a day. Work your way around your distractions and you will find a few effective ways to curb them.

Implement these strategies so you make a conscious effort to block your temptations. This is the best way to focus on your work and concentrate on the bigger picture.

10: Stop Working during Your Lunchbreak

Working during your lunch break does not only make you antisocial, it also affects your focus, creativity, and focus. Your body gets tired from working for too long and demands some rest. If you deprive it of that, your body and mind are likely to suffer. Research proves that taking a midday break helps you rejuvenate (physically and mentally) which improves your focus and productivity.

If you habitually work for 6 to 8 hours straight and eat a sandwich at your desk instead of going to the lunchroom or outside for some fresh air and a bite to eat, you are likely to feel dull, dreary, and exhausted too quickly.

Give your body and mind a well-deserved break at lunchtime by going out for a stroll, sitting at the cafeteria or a park, and having your lunch in quiet or in the company of a few friends. This practice keeps you from feeling emotionally and physically drained thus improving your focus and efficiency.

Even with killer focus, there are times when you will forget to do your important chores. That happens mainly because we have so many chores to attend to that we forget to pay attention to what is important. This bad habit lowers your productivity and your chances of achieving your goals.

The next chapter throws light on a few amazing ways to manage this habit and amplify your output.

Remember Your Tasks in 4 Simple Ways

Its 4pm and you just realized you had an important meeting to attend at 2pm. You are about to call the client and apologize for missing the meeting and just as you are about to, you remember you have to attend your daughter's recital at 4:30pm and the venue is about 50 minutes away from your office. Yikes! You better get going.

If you often forget to attend to important chores on time, you will feel connected to this scenario. Not doing tasks on time often stems from not remembering to do them. This habit is one you need to improve if you truly want to be the boss of your life and build a happy, meaningful, and successful life. Do not worry; this habit, like the others we have discussed, is changeable provided you are committed to changing and are ready to implement the strategies discussed below.

11: Create a To-Do List

Failing to recall what you ought to do at 9am and missing out on important chores every other day is a habit you must overcome so you can steadily move towards your goals and complete every chore that leads you to the fulfillment of your goals. A great hack that provides a nice fix to this problem is making a to-do list.

Each night before going to bed, plan what you intend to do the next day and prepare a concise To-do list that serves as a reminder of that plan. This ensures that on the next day, you do not waste time planning and organizing your schedule, make good use of your time, and get straight to action the next morning.

Write all the important tasks in bold and give them first priority on the list so you attend to them first, which as you can guess, shall increase your productivity. Make several hard copies of the To-do list and pin them up on your fridge, dining table, etc. In addition, have soft copies of the To-do list on your phone and laptop so that no matter where you go, you have your handy list with you.

12: Set Alarms

For extremely important tasks you cannot afford to miss, tasks such as being part of a board meeting or attending your son's graduation ceremony, set alarm reminders on your phone and computer. Having multiple reminders and alarms related to extremely high priority tasks ensures you never miss them and balance your work and family life well.

13: Create a Daily Calendar

You can also create your daily calendar to help you stay up to date with different tasks assigned for a certain day. Create a list of the tasks you plan to finish in a week and then assign them different days and times of the week. Make columns for started tasks, the completed ones, those under progress, and those you have put on pending.

Every morning, go through this calendar so you can figure out what you need to do that day. Look at your calendar once before going to bed so you can update it and get a clearer picture of your performance.

This calendar would look as follows.

Day	Task	Started and Finished at	**Completed**	**Work-in-Progress**	**Pending**	Postponed to a Later Date
Monday						
Tuesday						
Wednesday						
Thursday						
Friday						
Saturday						
Sunday						

This calendar has helped me remember chores, do them on time, and stay focused. I am sure it will do wonders for you too.

14: Ask a Friend to Remind You

Another effective way to ensure you stop forgetting your tasks is to seek help from a trusted, supportive friend/relative/family member. Give a list of your important tasks for the week to a friend with good memory and ask that friend to send you a message or give you a short call to remind you of those tasks. This is a good way to ensure you follow your To-do lists and pay heed to your daily calendar.

With these 4 simple hacks, you will definitely stay on the top of your tasks and will complete your work on time. In addition to practicing all the strategies discussed thus far, you also need to implement several other strategies that skyrocket your productivity.

Let us discuss those in the next chapter.

Chapter 11: Seven And Eight, You're Doing Great

Step Seven and Eight on Overcoming Procrastination

Step Seven: Forgive Yourself

Step seven, forgive yourself. This has to be the most important step. You must learn how to forgive yourself if things do not pan out how you want them. Everyone, including you, makes mistakes in life. No one is perfect. So, if you can effectively forgive yourself, then you will be on the road to overcoming anything you set in front of you. No one can complete everything one hundred percent of the time. It is you that needs to remind yourself of that. You need to remember, if you do the best you can, then no one will be able to stand in your way.

One of the first steps to overcoming procrastination is learning to forgive yourself. You do things you will never be able to overcome, but the thing is to move forward and past that. One situation does not dictate who you are as a person. Instead, how you tackle that situation does. You can allow it to trample on your; beat you down until you are nothing, but where would you get by allowing that? Who would you be afterward when you allow that to happen? There are many things you can be in life, but a person who gives up should not be one of them. Prosper from your mistakes, but do not allow them to reflect who you are as a person. Allow them to mold them into the person you want to become.

So, take this time to forgive yourself. It could be for something that was not in your power, or it could be for something that is. Either way, forgive yourself for it. Allow your mind to forgive you for something that you can no longer change. That is the only way you are going to take a step forward and overcome procrastination. Because when you forgive yourself, you will be able to conquer anything in your way. You just have to succumb to the fact you failed. I know it is hard, but everyone does it. We are all failures at one point in our lifetime. The only way you can break the habit, so to say, is by forgiving yourself for your actions and bracing yourself for the future.

Step Eight: Reward Yourself

There are many things you can do for this step, and yes, this is my favorite of them all by far. In this step, you will be able to reward yourself for overcoming procrastination and getting what you need to get done, completed. There are many ways you can reward yourself, and I will list them below. Some of these you may not have heard of, but now that you do, you will find you want to try them out.

So here are various ways you can reward yourself for overcoming procrastination:

•Take yourself out to breakfast. Allow yourself to rest and take in everything around you.

•Goof off online. Yes, this is intentional. Take a few hours to surf your favorite website, grab a movie online and watch it. Anything your heart desires, you can do with this time to yourself.

- Try retail therapy (Controlled). In doing this, you will walk from store to store, seeing things that you want to own for yourself. You will not actually buy these items, but with the next step, this one will become clearer as to why you would do this.
- Procrastination Jar. Yes, in this one you will reward yourself with money. It will be your own money going into the jar, but it is all the same. Every time you finish a project, assignment, or task—take money out of your wallet and put it into the jar. Once you have enough saved up, then you can retail therapy shop for real. You can buy the items that were on your eye previously, feeling refreshed because you know you worked hard for it.
- Buy yourself flowers. You will find that the sight of them will automatically make you a happier person. They are beautiful, which makes the world around you seem brighter.
- Get out of town. There may be an area in the state you are residing in that you have

always wanted to visit. Well, after everything is said and completed, go. Take your trip and allow nothing else to occupy your mind. You will find in doing this, that you are more refreshed and ready to tackle the next obstacle when you return. This is known as a 'reboot' if you will. It allows your mind to focus on nothing else than what you are doing at that given time.

You will see by rewarding yourself that you will be more prone to finish your tasks on time. Procrastination will cease to exist as long as you feel as if you are getting something out of it. It may not be much, but at least it is something. Your outlook on life will be much clearer than what it was originally, and you will also find yourself happier, more refreshed if you take the time for yourself.

Chapter 12: Morning Rituals For Happiness And Satisfaction

Victoria Durnak, a German writer, once said, "The silence in the morning holds lots of expectations and is more hopeful than the silence at night."

This quote highlights the importance of doing something useful in the morning: because it is the best time of day to be hopeful for something great. Hope will always bring a smile to your face.

In this chapter, we shall discuss various morning rituals that foster happiness, hope, and satisfaction:

1: Plan Something to Look Forward To

Begin your happy morning routine a night before by planning something to look forward to in the morning. Research shows that anticipation acts as a powerful happiness booster.

When you plan something a night before, you wait in anticipation and once you perform the task, you get 2 for the price of 1: joy from the activity, and joy from anticipation of the activity.

The activity you plan does not have to be something elaborate. It can be something as simple as waking up 15 minutes early to fix your spouse a surprise breakfast in bed, watching the sunrise, or buying your favorite coffee as you head to work on time. However, be sure to plan this a night before.

2: Practice Mindfulness

One of the best ways to start your morning is by practicing mindfulness. Mindfulness is the process of being fully aware of your thoughts, feelings, and the present moment without judgment.

Mindfulness is a type of meditation that frees your mind from unnecessary clutter, relaxes you, and makes you happy and stress-free. This practice does not have to take 30 minutes of your time; all you need is 5-10 minutes of peace and quiet. Practice the following exercise as part of your morning ritual daily:

Mindfulness Breathing

Sit on a chair or simply lie down.

After a few deep breaths, bring your focus towards the movement of your breath; focus on the inhalation and exhalation of air from your nostrils or the rising and falling of your chest as you breathe.

As you concentrate on your breath, your mind will start to wander. Without judging your thoughts, simply observe them for a few seconds and bring your attention back to you breathing.

Practice mindfulness breathing for 5-10 minutes daily in the morning.

Once you start to practice mindfulness regularly, apply it to other areas of your morning as well. For instance, while cooking breakfast, pay attention to every step. Mindfulness will fully relax you and enhance your mood.

When the beginning of your day is great, the rest of the day will be great as well. Moreover, this practice helps you become aware of your thoughts. This makes it easier to discern negative thoughts from positive ones and focus more on the healthy thoughts that make you feel positive and happy.

3: Manage Your Mood

According to research, your morning mood sets the mood for the rest of your day. Hence, as part of your morning routine, manage your mood when you wake up. You can manage your mood with a few simple and easy steps:

The moment you wake up, greet yourself by saying, "Good morning (name), how are you, today?" Doing this subconsciously tells your brain you are important and worthy of being greeted.

Practice affirmations when you wake up. An affirmation is a positive statement repeated aloud or subconsciously. Repeat the following affirmations when you wake up, "Today is going to be a great day. I will make my dreams come true. I will accomplish the goals I have set for today." Repeat this at least 5-10 times and you will feel an instant positive change of mood. Create affirmations focused on anything you want to achieve or improve on, things such as confidence, self-esteem, happiness, and self-acceptance.

Walk to the mirror and smile at yourself for at least 30 seconds. Smile with awe, gratitude, and love. Tell yourself how much you love yourself. This is a clever way of designating some quality 'me time' to your morning routine. Unbelievably, 30 seconds of self-love adds a lot to your goal of becoming a happy person and gives a great start to your day.

Simple actions like kissing your spouse, your children, or your parents as you wake up also help manage your mood and set the tone for the rest of the day.

Avoid These Rituals

Just like there are rituals you should practice to manage your mood, there are certain things you should avoid simply because they ruin your mood:

Avoid checking your e-mails first thing in the morning. There will be plenty of time to do that when you get to work. Studies show that when you check your e-mail first thing in the morning, you stress out because your mind has barely woken up yet.

Also, avoid using social media forums soon after waking up because doing so shifts your focus from yourself to others and often stresses you.

4: Practice Gratitude

Another great morning ritual is to practice gratitude because it reminds you of all the things you are grateful for, which brings a smile to your face. Here is how you can practice gratitude:

In a journal, list all things you are grateful for. For instance, if you recently delivered a great presentation, be grateful for this. If an elderly stranger smiled at you after you helped her/him cross the road, be grateful. Listing down everything (big and small) that has made you happy will give a great start to your day because you will begin your day with hope.

Say thank you to your spouse, mother, father, children, or siblings for always being there for you, for taking care of you, and for loving you unconditionally. Thank the universe for your amazing family, your car, your house, your job, and your amazing life.

When you get to work, thank one of your colleagues for being an amazing co-worker and for always having your back. Bringing a smile to others will make you immensely happy.

5: Practice Self-love

Lastly, practice self-love as part of your morning routine because it will make you happy. Here are a few things you can do to practice self-love:

Spend time alone reflecting on your thoughts and emotions. Instead of indulging in negative self-talk, write down all your accomplishments, abilities, and qualities in a journal.

Listen to your favorite music, read a few pages of your favorite book, or watch a re-run of your favorite comedy show.

Think of all your recent accomplishments or anything nice about yourself and appreciate yourself. For instance, if your skin looks fresh, say, "Wow, I have such smooth and glowing skin." Such appreciative talk boosts your self-esteem and you love yourself unconditionally.

Add these morning rituals to your morning routine and everyday will be as great as the previous one.

Chapter 13: Extra Habits To Make Your Morning Routine Even Peppier

We have discovered the perfect blueprint for that morning routine of yours and also seen exactly how we can ensure that we stick to the plan and make it a habit so it becomes every bit the morning ritual we hope it will be. Of course, there are plenty of other additional habits that you could incorporate into that ritual of yours – little habits that will go a long way in ensuring that your morning routine packs a punch! Let's take a look at them to see how we can make that morning routine of ours even peppier than it already is!

Some extra habits to incorporate into that morning routine of yours

Let the sunshine into your room

Getting up in the morning to sunlight is far more effective than waking up to darkness, where it comes to getting a great start to your day. You will find yourself far fresher and a great deal more invigorated if you allow that sunlight to filter in through your windows first thing in the morning. So, open your shades and let the light come in and see how your spirits are lifted – let the sunshine into your room and consequently into your life as well!

Go to bed at the same time every night

First of all, you have to ensure that you get at least 7 hours of sleep every night. It's best if you get 8, but 7 is pretty good as well. So, when you go to sleep you need to know that you are getting the designated hours of sleep that you are aiming at. It also helps if you go to bed at the same time every night. That way you won't be stretching that waking up time of yours to later in the morning and your routine will not be disturbed in the slightest.

Use your commute well

The fact that you have a morning routine in place to ensure that you do all the things that are important to you first thing in the morning does not mean you don't have time for other things, like checking your social media accounts. While you have ensured that such activities are not part of your main circle of activities in the morning, you could always do them on the go, whilst on your way to work. So, check your Facebook on the bus or read the paper in the train; that way you will find that you have time for everything without having wasted any time at all.

\# Don't hit that snooze button!

One of the most common mistakes people make in the morning is to hit that snooze button on the alarm. This is not the best way to start your morning, as it will only leave you feeling lethargic. The best way to get up is as soon as the alarm goes off, so ensure that you do away with the snooze feature altogether.

\# Take out your clothes for the following day the night before

The last thing you want to be in the morning is to find yourself harried, and that is exactly what will happen if you find yourself in a dilemma as to what you are going to wear to work. The best way to avoid this conundrum is to take out the clothes you intend to wear the coming day, the night before. When you do this you will find that you don't get that calm state of mind you have worked so diligently to achieve in the morning, disturbed by the mere act of choosing what to wear on that particular day.

Switch on your phone only when you are ready to leave for work

One of the most common temptations we all give in to practically every waking hour of our lives, is to fidget with those cell phones of ours. In fact, we waste a lot of time surfing social networking sites; time that could be very well spent doing more constructive things, like sticking to that morning routine of ours. Yes, this could very well be one of the reasons one ends up not sticking to that morning routine, after all, so ensure that your mobile phone is only switched after you have left the home.

Go for a leisurely walk amidst nature

You might have incorporated that brisk walk as a part of that morning schedule of yours, but a leisurely walk in the park where there is a lot of greenery around, could also do wonders to your state of mind in the morning. Perhaps you could do yoga in the park and then simply walk around, taking in the sights and smells around you. You will see that you feel much better than you already do, and take that yoga high to an altogether new dimension.

Make sure there is a place for everything

Just like you would have ensured that you don't waste any time on what should really be a rather simple process where it comes to selecting your clothes for the day, you don't wish to waste any time searching for things like your car keys and wallet. These are the things that you know you will need on a daily basis, so ensure that they have a special place where you keep them so you can remember where they are and not waste any time scrounging around searching for them.

Let the music play

Listening to music, especially music of the peppy kind is a great way to start that morning of yours. You could do this when you are getting dressed or even while you are in the shower. Make sure you only play the kind of music that gets you in the mood – calming music is not the ideal choice, unless you are using it to meditate. So, let the music play and watch those blues (if you have any) melt away!

Read

A lot of times we find that we simply do not have any time to read (something we have been planning to do for a very long time) simply because we are too tired after work. Well, you know when you're going to be least tired – in the morning, of course! So, take the time to read something nice in the morning. This is not to be confused with reading something inspirational as we have discussed before – by all means do that as well, but make sure you don't give up on the fine habit of reading great books!

Stretch

Whether you're going to the gym or doing yoga, you will find that stretching is most important where it comes to eliminating any injuries that might arise in the process of doing exercise. You don't wish to cause damage to your back and end up lying in bed for a large number of days just because you didn't invest two minutes of your day to the process of stretching, do you? Yes, all it takes is two minutes and you will be guaranteed to prevent yourself from undue injuries to yourself.

Get creative

The morning is perhaps the time when creativity reaches an all time high; make sure you make the most of it by doing something constructive towards your aspirations – even if it is merely the process of brainstorming where it comes to your longstanding dream of staring a restaurant of your very own. Perhaps you are planning to write a book but find that you never have the time to do so; you could ensure that you get a few words down on paper first thing in the morning when your mind is freshest. You don't have to spend an inordinate amount of time on this – even fifteen minutes is enough!

Chapter 14: Set Up A Streamlined Workspace

Have you ever experienced wasting time looking for something inyour home or workspace? Has it happened to you more than once? Imagine spending 30 minutes per month with this problem...that would mean a total of 6 hours of wasted time within a year!

The only way to eliminate this issue is by ensuring that you know exactly where all your belongings are."But that's impossible!"some might argue. However, you can make this a reality by following these three steps:

Declutter viciously.

Your workspace should contain only the things that you immediately need within it. You need to eliminate everything else. The best way to declutter is by first removing all the items from the shelves, closets, drawers and tables, then placing them together into one pile.

Then, segregate them into two distinct piles: the items that serve a direct purpose in the space, and the items that do not. Spare items, such as extra pens, should be included in the latter pile. They will only add to the clutter because you never use them anyway.

After getting rid of the items that do not belong, place them in other areas of the house or office where they are used. Otherwise, you need to donate them or send them off to the recycle bin.

Assign a specific place for every item.

Next, you should decide where to put all the items that you currently use within that workspace. To help instill the habit of putting places back to where they belong, you can post labels on them.

For example, let's say you have three drawers: the leftmost one is where you want to keep your pens and sticky notes, the one in the middle is where you want to store your files and the one on the right is where you want to keep your gadgets. Using your sticky notes, label the one on the left "pens and sticky notes," and so on. Later on, when your mind and body are used to pulling the right drawers without checking the label, you can remove the notes.

Incorporate features that promote concentration.

Once you have decluttered and organized your workspace, you can become even more time efficient in it by adding details that will help you focus better there. For instance, it is essential for you to enclose your workspace to make it private. If it cannot be in a separate room, then use other barriers, such as room dividers or even curtains. You can also hang up a "do not disturb" sign.

Another common technique is to play instrumental music, or the ones without lyrics. Notice how it will dramatically improve your focus and at the same time drown out noise from the outside world.

Also, make it a habit to keep your workspace as bare as possible. The more items there are on your desk, the easier it is to get distracted. The only items that you should put on your desk are the ones related to your task at hand; all else needs to be stored away.

As you continue to streamline your workspace, you will eventually learn how to make it more conducive for productivity. Some people like to add a few touches, such as a potted plant or some coffee incense to make it cozy. You can make adjustments along the way as long as you have finished the three steps mentioned.

Chapter 15: How To Organize Your Priorities

The most effective method to organise your workload

The organisation is an expertise that is acquired out through the span of months; in some cases years. It can be hard to study great organisation simply in light of the various exercises we are confronted with which require special thinking in the approach, and this is incredibly time-consuming.

Making achievement a habit is difficult. Not incomprehensible. In today's expert world, confidence alongside diligent work and determination will advance in your desired direction. Sorting out our workload is of prime significance, to allow acknowledgement of our expert and individual objectives. Sorting out your time has a considerable measure to do with the benefit of your company or accomplishment of your project. It is fundamental to arrange your office time and individual time independently for exceptional utilisation.

Organisation implies the capability to organise:

Tasks- Preparation of a work schedule is the key to remaining on track; breaking large assignments into small undertakings and its satisfaction will give a feeling of advance and accomplishment to finish next task.

Folders and Records - Keep one hour for every week to sort out your folders and records. Title and flag them all together in order of significance, this recovers the data rapidly and increase effectiveness in office. Utilise coded shading tags if necessary.

Time - Set a limit for each assignment. Audit your work schedule each day morning and assess at night. This will help to share out the vital time to each project. In the office, apportion time for telephone calls, meetings and answering to mails and stick to it. With experience, one will understand that - the better you arrange your life; the better you have an effective yield in office.

Your considerations/feelings - Personal conceptualising helps in sorting out contemplations and feelings and keeps you far from tension and sets you up for taking care of future circumstance better. For arranging thoughts and feelings, scrutinise your triumph and last disappointment. This examination will decide the elements for achievement and disappointment.

Best Tips

1. Keep a period journal of all exercises - Prepare your work schedule according to need and execute likewise.

2. Oversee viable communication - Keep a clean inbox with classified folders for different mail.

3. Get ready ahead of time for meetings- Ensure a productive return.

4. Prioritise - For various projects close by and various tasks to accomplish - organise and settle on a timeline to keep you on top of the things.

5. Assign tasks to skilled individuals - Saves you time and vitality.

Overseeing workloads adequately will keep you free from anxieties and will help you to perform better in the workplace and will eventually help you accomplish your coveted personal and professional goals. The organization is the way to overseeing workloads and will enhance business execution if done viably.

Step by step instructions to Prioritise Work When Everything Is #1

All projects—particularly substantial, complex projects—require precise priorities. Simpler said than done. You can rely on technical projects, regardless of how all around arranged, to include change orders, re-prioritization and the customary appearance of surprises. It's recently the usual order of things.

Knowing how to organise function influences the achievement of your project, the engagement of your group and your part as a pioneer.

One of the greatest difficulties for project directors and pioneers is precisely prioritising the work that matters daily. Regardless of the possibility that you have the best project administration programming on the planet, you're the person who enters data into the tool. Furthermore, you would prefer not to fall into the part of crying "top priority" for each other project that needs to be addressed. You must be determined and have the right sort of project insight to guarantee that no one's taking a shot at yesterday's priority. It adopts a considerable measure of practice to get this right.

To help you deal with your group's workload and hit the deadline, here are six stages to organising projects that have a considerable measure of moving parts.

Gather a rundown of every one of your assignments. Pull together all that you could consider completing in a day. Try not to stress over the request or the number of things in upfront.

Recognise urgent versus important. The next stride is to check whether you have any assignments that need quick attention. We're discussing work that, if not finished before the day's over or in the following a few hours, will have serious negative results (missed customer deadline; missed production or discharge period, and so on.). Verify whether any high-pre conditions depend on you completing a bit of work now.

Access value. Next, search for your critical work and distinguish what conveys the most astounding an incentive to your business and association. As a general practice, you need to perceive precisely which sorts of tasks have top priority over the others. For instance, concentrate on customer projects before internal work; setting up the new CEO's PC before re-configuring the database; replying support tickets before composing training materials, et cetera. Another approach to evaluating esteem is to take a look at what number of individuals are affected by your work. When all is said in done, the more people included or impacted, the higher the stakes.

Arrange tasks by assessed effort. If you have assignments that appear to tie for priority standing, check their appraisals, and begin on whichever one you think will require the most effort to finish. Efficiency specialists recommend the strategy of beginning the lengthier assignment first. If you sense that you can't concentrate on your meatier projects before you complete the shorter task, then run with your gut and do that. It can persuade to mark a little undertaking off the list before jumping into deeper waters.

Be adaptable and versatile. Vulnerability and change are given. Realise that your priorities will change, and frequently when you when you least expect them to. Be that as it may, here's the trick—you additionally need to remain concentrated on the tasks you're committed to finishing.

Know when to cut. You most likely can't get to everything on your list. After you organise your chores and take a look at your appraisals, cut the rest of the tasks from your outline, and concentrate on the needs that you know you should and can finish for the day. At that point take a full breath, make a leap and be prepared for anything.

Chapter 16: Organizing Yourself And Your Mind

Organization can be the key to success. If you go into the office of the highly successful, you won't see trash, clutter, dirt and dust scattered throughout – you will see a clean, neat and organized office space. With the exception of work clutter, an organized desk can help you easily locate anything you need and can also give you a more relaxed feeling because you have room to spread out and do what you need to do without requiring much effort in the way of moving stuff around.

When attempting to organize yourself, you must first figure out what exactly is cluttered. For anyone who lives in a cluttered household, clean it up and organize it. Put things away that are sitting out, buy attractive containers that easily slide in, out and under different types of furniture so easy organization. People don't realize the volume of effect a clean home environment can have on your mindset. Coming home to a house that has clothes on the floor, dishes scattered around, trash on the ground and clutter on the surfaces can keep you from feeling that peaceful "being at home" feeling that everyone deserves to have when they walk through their front door.

Organizing your home can take as little as a day depending on the amount of work involved. Almost as soon as your home is decluttered and organized, you will notice a difference in your mindset. You will feel accomplished and feel a sense of importance, which is the kind of attitude you need when moving forward on tasks that you usually put off to the last minute. Organizing yourself and your routine can help a lot too. Getting out of bed in a hurry, throwing clothes on and running out the door is no way to start the morning. You are already starting your morning off stressed and late which is the exact behavior you are trying to avoid bringing into your life and work. Instead, pack your lunch the night before, pick out the clothes and outfit you are going to wear, set out your socks, shoes and undergarments, so everything is easily accessible in the morning. Some people even go so far as to lie out on the counter, everything they use in the morning such as face wash, makeup (if applicable), toothbrush, deodorant, perfume or cologne and jewelry.

Having everything set out in the morning allows you to wake up prepared for the morning routine and with little stress involved. Giving yourself an extra half hour in the morning can mean the difference between starting out stressed and starting off on the right foot. Having coffee and breakfast set out to start in the morning can also make your morning routine smoother and more pleasurable and may even leave time for some morning relaxation before heading into work. People often overlook the importance of relaxing while others take advantage of relaxing to the extreme, resulting in missing or putting off tasks that need to be done. Stress needs to be avoided with relaxation, but too much relaxation can cause stress all on its own. It's a vicious cycle that needs to be balanced to avoid malfunction.

A messy car is also another place that organization needs to occur. Everyone loves new cars because they are clean, fresh smelling and decluttered. When beginning to organize your life, one of the first places you should start is your car. You use your car to take you everywhere — some people spend their entire job in their car, driving around. Having a car that is clutter free and smells nice can help you stay relaxed throughout the day. Again, the goal here is consistency and keeping you in the right mindset to stay organized and on time and tackle the tasks you tend to put off.

For woman, decluttering your purse and wallet is a rejuvenating feeling. Throwing away stuff in your purse such as wrappers, receipts you don't need and used coupons not only makes your purse cleaner, it also makes it less stressful to go digging in your bag for your keys or your wallet and having to sift through a bunch of unnecessary items in order to find what you are looking for. As I stated before, little things like this we overlook on a daily basis but they add up and cause us high amounts unnecessary stress that can have ripple effects in our life that we don't even realize. Having clutter everywhere can lead to stress that can lead to behaviors like procrastination, which can lead to even more stress.

Decluttering your mind is a whole new, daunting task. To focus on your mind, you need to get your environment under control. Decluttering and organizing your environment will help your thoughts to stay clean and organized. Think of it like this, if you leave bills to pay on the table, an empty plate, a sock and a pencil on the table, coming home and seeing the table will automatically make you think the following things: "Oh, I need to pay those bills," (money stress), "I need to do dishes," (household chore stress), "I need to find the other sock. I need to do laundry," (more household chore stress),

"I need to put that away," (organization stress). So, walking through the door and looking at the table you already have a minimum of four different, slight stressors that will pile on top of each other and continue to do so if the remainder of your house looks like that.

Another example would be trying to meditate when someone across from you is screaming. In order to meditate, you need peace and quiet in order to allow the peace and quiet to enter your mind. Having someone screaming makes peace and quiet impossible, and therefore, meditation cannot be achieved. So, after organizing your environment, you can begin to organize your mind. The mind is one of the last few organs that we know the least amount about. Only in the recent decades as a significant amount of research and studies have been conducted on brain research.

Organizing the mind can seem daunting, and it very well may be, but it is also highly possible to do effectively. Organizing your mind can begin after your environment is organized, and should then be addressed by whom you spend your time with. Having a healthy relationship within your family and your love life (significant other) can greatly reduce stress and help keep you in the right mindset. Being around some who is going a thousand miles an hour all the time can be mentally exhausting and physically demanding. These details may seem ridiculous, but before judgment and criticism if given, put your whole heart into making these changes and see how much better you feel.

Organizing your mind can be stressful, but it is easily combatted with simple ways to organize. Making lists, meditation and exercise can help keep your mind organized and focused, helping you to succeed in all aspects of your work and (if applicable) school life. Keeping yourself in the right state of mind can be the difference between living happily and productively or living life self-loathing and procrastinating.

Organizing can be one of the most difficult things for us to do because a lot of us are set in our ways and don't like change. A lot of us claim to have a type of "messy order," but we don't realize the negative impact it is actually having on our mental health. Seeing so much clutter at one time, even if we aren't consciously thinking about it, our subconscious is being bombarded with different stimuli and thoughts that will come up later. Keeping yourself organized inside and out makes for the best results in attempting to organize your mind and your thoughts.

At night, a lot of people have a difficult time falling asleep because of all the thoughts floating around in their mind. There are different techniques you can use to "organize" these thoughts while you are lying with your eyes closed in bed. Sometimes people fall asleep while performing these exercises, which is wonderful because that is what they are intended for. You can begin by closing your eyes and taking a deep breath. Picture two bins, one is for things you can change, and one is for things that you cannot change. Picture your thoughts like a swirling cloud above these two bins with you standing down below as a stick figure in between the bins. Reach up and grab the first, most pressing thought in your mind, and sort it into the bins. Do this for all the thoughts, realizing that both bins, in the end, will be considered trash because you cannot change what you cannot change and you cannot change what you can change at that exact moment in time.

Having thoughts that keep you up at night can be an easy fix if you focus. If at any point in time you lose focus during the exercise, start over from the beginning again. Before you know it, you will be waking up in the morning refreshed and hopefully slightly less stressed than you were the night before. There are so many ways to combat behaviors in our lives that lead to certain actions like procrastination. The key is to identify these and eliminate them.

Chapter 17. Finding Inspiration

We all need to have some form of inspiration in our lives. If you catch public transport, why not get yourself a great biography of someone who you admire. Going through the pages of a book can cut that journey in half and get you there filled with the kind of inspiration that makes you want to work hard to achieve and to be like your hero in life.

Other forms of inspiration are those of escape. Have you got a favorite author? What about reading something that fills you with hope and happiness? There's nothing wrong with reading poetry on the tram or reading up on something that interests you. You don't get paid enough to give this time to your work and should make the most of it.

If you are driving to work, why not invest in a tape to help you to practice a new language. The miles go by much faster when you are feeding the brain with something new and languages make an ideal example of the kind of things you can introduce, even when you are driving. You are less likely to get worked up if there is a bottleneck and you are stuck in traffic and, at the same time, you are giving yourself something very enjoyable and inspiring to listen to.

Music can do the same thing, but remember, this is morning. Try not to choose music that is too fast or too hectic. The idea is to make the journey to work inspirational, rather than fraught. Thus, choose music that inspires you and that perhaps you don't get a chance to listen to at home. One driver I know who has to drive in the rush hour daily catches up with listening to opera, since no one in his family appreciates his choice of music and it's too important to him to let go of and stop enjoying.

There is inspiration all around you. You need to let that inspiration into your mind to take the place of the banality of having to drive the same way every day. Even on a commute in the train, these days, there's nothing wrong with listening to your music and investing in an MP3 player may be the best investment that you make. However, be aware that it's very easy to be tempted to sing with your MP3 player and that other passengers may not appreciate your version of what it is that you are listening to!

If you live somewhere where there is a wonderful view, this gives you a great opportunity to come up close and personal with inspiration first thing in the morning. For example, watching a sunrise in the morning can truly get you close to your spiritual side, as can sitting outside and looking over the valleys below and getting back in touch with your inner self.

Above the place where I stayed in Tibet, there was a hill I found on which to meditate in the mornings. Not only were the sunsets the brightest red I have ever seen, but what struck me about a scene like this is how it inspires you and brings you back to the reality of life, instead of being fed constant advertisements from the TV. You are surrounded by nature and suddenly you realize how small you are. If you are wondering how feeling small can make you feel spiritual or be in any way good, you have to understand the importance of humility.

Humility puts everything into perspective. It shows you how small you are in comparison with everything that you see, but it also lets you know that the smallness doesn't make you less important. A tree without its twigs isn't the same. The sea without each grain of sand is not the same. The small parts that make up our world are each important in their own way. What it does is lift this veil of materialism and make you feel happy with who you are and that's very inspiring.

Even if you don't meditate in the most inspirational of places, it's nice to look out of the window or step outside and be inspired. Even in a town garden, you can be inspired by seeing the early morning mist settling its dew drops on the plants in the garden and making it appear as though there are diamonds hanging on the cobwebs of the night.

The morning is such an inspiration to me since opening my life to the wild and appreciating what each day brings about as a matter of course. It's never predictable. It's always different. You just need to look beyond the obvious to see it and that's what I love about mornings. People who stay in bed in the mornings often make the noises that they disapprove of my early morning demeanor, but when they see how positive I am about life, they also want to learn how to get that positivity themselves.

If you can make the morning itself inspire you, you wake up to a wonderful feeling that today is a fresh day and a new start, and that it gives you the potential to be a better human being than you were yesterday. That's truly inspiring and something that you don't need to be told. You simply feel it inside you and it makes you very positive about life, as you get ready to face another day — no matter what negative things that day ahead may hold.

If you face all of your adversities with the happy heart, things suddenly change and you feel very in control of your own life and your own destiny and can achieve anything.

Chapter 18: 5 Little Golden Nuggets

5 actionable gold nuggets which you can do it right now

1. Find a partner or buddy who can help you stop procrastinating. Tell that person that you will give him $100 or do him a favor each time you miss a day of work, school, etc. or you do not complete a task or project. Make sure that you commit to this and fulfill your promise.

2. Set a reminder. Each morning upon waking up, you should check your planner or to-do list. Make this a habit. Do not get out of bed until you find out what you need to do for the day. You can make things easier by putting your planner or to-do list on your bedside table. This way, you can easily reach for it in the morning.

3. Stick a note on your computer. This note should contain all the reminders, such as sending or replying to an important e-mail, finishing the client's website, downloading a document, etc. It is easy to forget these things the moment

you go online and log on into your social media account. You can get swayed by the notifications and forget why you logged on in the first place.

4. Choose a task that you are supposed to do and focus on it alone for ten minutes. Do not do anything else. When the time is up, you can stop doing it and do something else.

5. Whenever you feel an urge to switch tasks, you should take a break. Pause for a while and see if the urge goes away. Usually, urges like this go away after a few seconds or minutes. When it is gone, you can go back to doing your task. You should not allow yourself to switch tasks until you have completed what you set out to do in the first place.

Time Management Training Game

Time management is essential in being productive and getting things done. The following game would greatly help to enhance the skill.

You Can Have My Procrastination

You Can Have My Procrastination is taken from Dragoş V. Iliescu's Time Management Training Games. Its main objective is to help the participants know about the causes of their procrastination and then find the appropriate solutions for them.

You can practice this training method with your friends or a group of other people who suffer from this same bad habit - procrastinate. It can be done by four to sixteen participants. However, you need to have an even number of participants because this technique requires pairs.

You do not need any materials, and it only takes half an hour. You can also do this training activity anywhere. So, even if you are busy, you can still do it. It does not take up much of your time. You can even do it in a public park or in your home.

Take note that you also need to have a moderator. This should be someone who is not biased and can provide encouragement. You can seek help from a therapist or counselor.

First of all, you and the other participants should be grouped and paired. You have to discuss with your partner the tasks that you have been putting off doing. Do not be shy to talk about it in detail. Usually, people forget to digest the details of their tasks that's why they are not able to pinpoint directly why they procrastinate.

For example, you may procrastinate reviewing for your Math exam, but you cannot pinpoint exactly why. If you look back and think of all the details involved, you may find out that you are procrastinating because you have failed a Math exam before and you are afraid to fail again.

Ask your partner to share his thoughts about your tasks and procrastination. Listen carefully and intently to his suggestions. Do not interrupt your partner and try to defend yourself. If you want to get better, you need to be open to criticisms. Listen to what other people have to say. They may see things that you cannot see because you are blindsided.

What does this mean? For example, you may be putting off reviewing for a Physics exam, not because you detest Physics or you are bad at it, but because you and your boyfriend had a fight a few days ago and you cannot bring your mind to focus on reviewing. You may think that this is a minor problem, but other people would see this at a different point.

You may not realize that you are already being verbally and emotionally abused, but other people can. Your bad relationship is affecting your studies, which is why you need to get out of it as soon as possible. Once you are out, you can move on and your mind is clearer.

Thus, you will be able to focus on your studies again. You will once again be motivated to review.

Of course, you should not be the only one talking. Your partner should also share his thoughts and feelings about his procrastination. Likewise, you should offer him advice that may be helpful. When your discussion is over, you should ask your partner how he felt about it and whether or not he thinks your suggestions are feasible and helpful.

You can ask the following questions for your debriefing:

What was it like to see from the perspective of other people?

Which tips do you find helpful in overcoming procrastination?

What techniques can you practice to refrain from procrastinating?

Chapter 19: Becoming A Procrastination Strategist

We're all guilty of having bad habits. We can have full control over them, we have the option of stopping them, they could hinder us from fortune, or they could entirely destroy our goals. Habits are what keep us ticking and what feeds into the autopilot we live on. By choosing to be creatures of habit rather than conscious control we're enabling ourselves to be procrastinators. Basically, habits can make or break us.

Procrastination is self-inflicted. It's a habit because it is something you can control. If you choose to stop procrastination right now, then you've decided to improve your life.

It is interesting to think how we can make things happen just by using simple mind over matter.

Habits of Successful People

Successful people all have one thing in common – they get things done. I'm not saying they don't procrastinate but they have habits that promote rather than hinder their success and usually have a routine arranged around these habits to keep pushing them towards (or beyond) their goals.

The Now Habit

Successful people have formed a habit for themselves to reach decisions punctually and to progress. You keep saying you'll do better in your job, you keep saying you'll start eating better and starting to lose weight, you keep saying you will stop multitasking but you never actually do it. You don't take that final step and make a decision. Successful people are decisive. They know that as long as they continue to take decisions they are making progress.

You've probably heard the term that failure is simply one less path to try on the road to success. It's true. By failing, you found a way that won't work, freeing you up to try another way which will. Fear is a powerful motivator, and if your procrastination is due to fear of success you're going to have difficulty getting past this unless you choose to be more decisive. Make a habit of avoiding gray areas – decisions are yes or no, with no exceptions.

Portioning

If you're addicted to success or scared of it portioning your tasks makes them much more achievable. Rather than looking at your entire to do list start splitting it up – what needs to be done today, what needs to be done before lunch etc. If necessary you can set yourself an alarm to let you know that time has passed or that you should be finished with something. The key with portioning is not to multi-task because it destroys your focus.

Most successful people are focused, they dedicate their energies to the task at hand without worrying about anything else. This means they're less distracted and more likely to finish.

Another reason portioning is good for success is because you are being successful. By achieving small successes on the way to the final goal you keep moving forwards, and you also train yourself not to be so scared of success because you're already living in the "post-success" of your last success which makes it much less scary.

For goals to be successful they need to be S.M.A.R.T:

Specific – you have to have a specific goal e.g Become partner vs get promoted.

Measurable – can you set steps which show progress towards the goal eg, getting a management position then getting partner.

Achievable – a lofty goal sets yourself up for failure. The goal has to be something you have a legitimate chance of achieving.

Relevant – Like achievable, is there a reason you are pursuing this goal? Is it responsible for you to spend time on it?

Timed – can you set a time limit on the achievement to determine whether you're successful or not? e.g make partner by the time I'm 30.

This is part of determining whether your task and your goal is useful. Successful people use strategies like this to measure their progress and keep moving forwards.

Prioritizing

Effectively prioritizing your life means choosing to do the things that are important and sacrificing those that aren't. General Eisenhower was extremely good at this. He created a system to delegate and distribute all of his paperwork during WW2 so that he never missed anything and every piece was taken care of. You can only imagine how much that was. Think of any time you have prioritized, why did you make that decision? What made that task more important than any other? We use a simple process to consciously do this – we determine whether the task is important and whether it's urgent. Look at the table on the following page:

	Important	Not Important
Urgent	X	
Not Urgent		Y

Which task do you think is more likely to get done? X right? If you procrastinate then you're choosing Y. By deciding a task is both important and urgent it will get done. Perceived important is as important as actual importance because that's what motivates you to do it. By owning the behavior you can choose whether to do the task or put it off.

Tasks that are Important + Urgent = priority

Tasks that are Unimportant + Not Urgent = delegate to someone else or simply take them off your to-do list.

Any other task can be put off "for now".

The Pareto principal

When I started this book I told you I wasn't lazy, but we all love to be lazy so what if I told you you could be lazy and still get stuff done? This is called the Pareto Principal and it was created in 1906 by economist Vilafredo Pareto. He realized that wealth was distributed in Italy very unevenly and 80% of the people did most of the work but only 20% of the population owned 80% of the wealth between them. It's like having a group project where only one person pulls their weight but everyone still gets an A.

Looking at your to-do list and determining urgency and importance you can rank everything. The top 20% of that list is your actual to-do list, everything else isn't important and is just to be a "bonus" once you're done.

The Pareto principal also looks at risk, determine which items are more likely to get procrastinated on from the 20% and choose to prioritize those first.

Focusing your energies on this top 20% makes it more likely you'll knock off the important things first, but it doesn't stop the rest of the list being there. What this does is bring your stress level down by eliminating the most important and most pressing tasks and help you be more organized about your schedule.

Chapter 20: Being A More Productive Student

Studying involves a lot of work. School activities and homework don't seem to run out. You always have something to do. You always have something to read and you always have something to memorize. If you want to get high grades, you need to learn how to be more productive. It is the only way through which you can maximize the time you have in order to absorb all the information that you need to learn.

Here are some tips that can help you study more productively and more efficiently. These tips are simple but they can make a huge difference in helping you learn in a more efficient manner.

61. Study in an unfamiliar place

When you are in a place that you are familiar with, distractions can be more easily noticed. For example, at home, you might constantly stand up to do a chore or an errand. You might even drop your books for a long nap. At the library, your friends might distract you. If you are in an unfamiliar place, it is very unlikely that you will encounter anything that will distract you from your work. A coffee shop is usually an ideal place for studying. You can also study in parks and in other locations that can help you concentrate on your study material.

62. Say no to technology

Keep away your smartphone and close the window of your social media account. Technology has indeed given us numerous benefits, but unfortunately, it can also be a big source of distraction. You will be surprised by the amount of time you can spend in front of the computer. It will keep you away from your books and it will definitely eat up your study time. Try to keep your laptops and phones away when you are studying and you will be much more productive.

63. Reward yourself

It is always a good idea to reward your efforts. Set up rewards before you start studying. For example, "I'll eat this candy bar when I finish reading 30 pages" or "I'll take a five-minute rest when I finish this chapter". Reward yourself whenever you finish a certain milestone. Your rewards can be simple, but they will surely keep you going. They will help you read further and push yourself even when you are tired.

64. Have a reliable study buddy

This tip is not applicable for everyone. There are certain individuals who find this technique effective. Have a reliable study buddy who can help you understand your lessons. You can talk to each other about lessons and you can exchange ideas. A reliable study buddy can accompany you in coffee shops and you can share notes with each other. Just try to find someone who has the same study habits as you do.

65. Listen well in class

If you listen well in class, there is a possibility that you don't even need to study before an exam. All you have to do is review your notes. Listen to your professors and teachers. Try to really understand the ideas presented to you. If you comprehend the information you learn in class, you can get away with studying less when you are on your own.

66. Handwrite your notes

Studies show that handwriting information will make it easier to remember. It is a much more effective technique than typing, or worse, listening. Nothing beats the old school combo of pen and paper. If you actually use your hand to write down information, your brain will be able to remember more efficiently. So when you are in class, the best thing to do is to ditch your laptop and tablet and just write down everything instead.

67. Organize the information

Remembering can be so much easier if you know how to connect one idea to another. Whenever you learn something new, always connect it to something that you already know. This will make it easier for you to remember. In a sense, you should always create a mind map where everything you know is connected.

68. Teach other students

When you are teaching, you are presenting the information in your own way. Before you could actually teach anyone, you must understand the information first. Teaching can help you check if you understood the material enough. If you are having a difficult time presenting information, chances are, you did not completely understand what you learned.

69. Ask for help

This is a good habit that can help you as a student and even later in life. Don't hesitate to ask for help when you don't know what to do. More often than not, there are people who are more than willing to help you. A good student knows that there is nothing wrong with asking help from other people. It is a good practice that will allow you to learn from others.

70. Follow a study schedule

Create a study schedule that will allow you to manage your time as needed. Make sure to be aware of your exam schedule and all your requirement deadlines so that you can prepare as needed. It is a bad idea to just cram everything. If you do so, the information you learned will just stick to your short-term memory. In a sense, you don't really get to learn everything.

71. Make sure that your study area is comfortable

How you feel when you study will affect the way you absorb your reading material. If you feel uncomfortable, you will waste a lot of time getting comfortable. If you can't see the information clearly, you might have difficulty understanding what you read. Try to make sure that your study area is comfortable to avoid wasting time. In your home, assign a specific spot as your study area. Make sure that you have a comfortable desk, a comfortable chair and good lighting.

72. Read, read, read

When you read more, you know more. It is a good habit to pick up. You don't even have to read academic materials all the time. You can even read entertainment and fashion magazines if you want. The important thing is to get into the habit. Try to learn to love books. You never know when you can use the information you read.

73. Take occasional naps

As a student, you are probably used to all-nighters and long study sessions. Give yourself a break. Recharge by taking occasional naps. However, keep in mind that you should limit your power naps to fifteen minutes. Anything longer than that might make you lazy and even sleepier. Fifteen minutes is just the right time to give your energy enough boost and help you keep going.

74. Invest in school supplies

You will be surprised by how much a nice notebook or a nice pen can do for your learning. Aside from helping you learn in a more comfortable manner, you will also be more motivated to study if you have nice things around you. Invest in items that will inspire you to learn. Buy the things you need because they can help make studying a bit more bearable for you.

75. Practice speed-reading

Speed-reading is a technique that will help you absorb and understand information in a fast and efficient way. It is more than just mindless skimming. It is a skill that is worth learning, especially if you plan pursuing further studies that require a lot of reading. Invest time, money and effort in learning this skill and the way you absorb information will never be the same again.

76. Know your learning style

Different people have different learning styles. Are you a visual or an auditory learner? Do you know the most effective way for you to absorb information? Learn more about your learning style so that you will be able to absorb information completely. It is not wrong to experiment with various styles first, but eventually, you must be able to figure out what group you belong in. Know your style and be a more efficient learner.

77. Know the resources that are available at hand

You might end up spending so much time on things that don't need to be hard. If you know the available resources around you, you will find it easier to look for information that you might need in your study. Visit your library and browse the Internet. You should know the resources you can use as you learn. It will help you save a significant amount of time if you know where to look for the things you need.

78. Know when and how to use the Internet

In relation to the above tip, you should also learn how to use the Internet. The information that you will stumble upon in websites is endless. If you try to read everything, you will never finish. Also, you might miss out important stuff if you don't know how to look for information correctly. Maximize the search engine that you are using. Learn how to use keywords when you are searching for something.

How you use the Internet will greatly affect the results that you come up with.

79. Stay fit and healthy

When you are studying, you will be sitting most of the time. There is a good chance that you will have a sedentary lifestyle as you spend most of the time on a chair. Be conscious of this detrimental aspect of being a student. In your daily routine, always inject physical activities that can help you with your studies. Also, eat healthy food. There are certain kinds of food, like nuts and proteins, which are said to be directly related to brain improvement.

Choose your lifestyle wisely. A healthy lifestyle will much likely make you a more productive student.

80. Don't mindlessly memorize information

Keep in mind that studying is more than just memorizing. A good student will really try to comprehend and understand whatever material is given. When you are just memorizing what you read, you are not really learning because you are just reciting the information like a parrot. In a sense, you won't be able to use what you learn in a concretely productive way. On the other hand, if you understood what you read, you can be confident that you can use the knowledge and skills you acquired to help you in life.

Chapter 21: The Comfort Zone Fear Of Separation And Fear Of Intimacy

Procrastination can result in a lot more than offering protection to a person from judgment or providing a covert way in engaging in a battle. Postponement and delay can result in regulation of degree of closeness that is maintained by a person with others. It also preserves the interpersonal distance. Whenever people are not sure of their ideas or are not able to come up with one, they rely on others for help. This does not imply that you need to get feedback from others or brainstorm with someone. You can reply on the viewpoint of somebody else which can be incorporated in solving any problem.

This is when people may feel the presence of others to get going. They feel afraid that they would not be able to do anything without any partnership. Few people feel comfortable when they are under somebody else's wing. They are looking for a mentor, guide or a cheerleader who can help them feel safe. They avoid things that would propel them to the top where they feel too alone or separate from the rest.

Fear of Separation: I'll never walk alone

People may start procrastinating when they do not want to leave their bosses who mentored them at the workplace initially.

This can also be applicable to a person with whom they had serious relationship for the first time.

Procrastination sets in when they do not feel confident about surviving in an independent manner.

This is lamentable whenever one derives a little bit of guidance, nurturance, support or protection from a relationship.

The truth is that they are diminishing their lives by living in such relationships. They prefer to be with someone rather than remaining alone in the world.

The fear of separation prevents them from taking a break which would be in their best interests.

Some people utilize procrastination as a tool to push themselves into a deep hole so that people would come along and dig them out. They use procrastination when in an emergency to ask help from others. The ultimate rescue for such people is to make somebody else work for you. Procrastination is a burden as well as a companion for some in life. This keeps you from feeling abandoned or lonely in life as you are always busy with list of projects in your mind that you let neither go nor complete.

Fear of Intimacy: Too close for comfort

People who fear separation derive a great sense of security from remaining close. In contrast, people maintain a comfortable distance when they fear intimacy. Some people are under the assumption that remaining in relationships would drain all the energy from them. They fear that others would never feel satisfied and would keep demanding more and more from them. This may eventually end up depleting them.

Some procrastinators are under the assumption that at the culmination of all her effort and hard work, somebody else would end up taking all the credit.

The very thought of somebody else taking away the credit can be upsetting and painful to few.

They would rather give somebody else the opportunity for stealing what is rightfully theirs. Their sense of self is closely tied to their accomplishments.

They feel being robbed of their very identity when somebody steals the credit that they think that they deserve.

This is when people use procrastination as a tool for protecting themselves from being used by others.

Some people fear getting into relationships as they fear repeating past experiences that were not so good.

They worry that they would land in pressure upon getting into an intimate relationship. You fear revealing your dark side to people who may get closer to you.

People who have the tendency to avoid intimate relationships do not want to acknowledge how much they long intimacy.

They fear developing a close relationship as they may end up discovering how much needy they are emotionally.

Whether the anxiety is stemming from fear of intimacy or fear of separation, you use procrastination as a tool for maintaining the boundaries of your zone of comfort.

All relationships involve issues of intimacy and boundaries. The key lies in resolving the differences both individually and as a partner while in a relationship. Procrastination prevents you from growing as a person even though it helps you keep other people at a safe distance. It is essential to be both dependent and independent in a relationship. A relationship can be a reliable zone to seek comfort. It becomes more fulfilling when it encourages the development of each individual.

Chapter 22: Eliminating Procrastination

It is a common misconception that procrastination is caused by inherent laziness. Procrastination is a complex issue that is more often a symptom of avoidance, sensory overload, or indecision. Sometimes, your brain knows that you have X number of tasks to complete, and because it can't decide which one is best to start with, the end result is not working on any of them at all. At other times, there are simply too many options, and your brain freezes because it's overwhelmed. Fear and anxiety can also play huge roles in a person's tendency to chronically procrastinate. The ultimate cure for procrastination is working smarter, not working harder.

One thing that it's important to keep in mind is that different people procrastinate for different reasons. According to Dr. Joseph Ferrari, professor of psychology at De Paul University, there are three main types of chronic procrastinators. Arousal-type procrastinators wait until the last minute because they crave the excitement of working down to the wire. This is the type of procrastinator who's most likely to say they "work best under pressure." Avoidance-type procrastinators are paralyzed by their fear of failure. They are often very concerned with the opinions of others, to the point they'd rather do no work at all and appear lazy than turn in work that's judged unworthy. Finally, decisional procrastinators are unable to choose a course of action and, because of that, get stuck circling the problem without ever doing anything about it.

Granted, not everyone is a chronic procrastinator. Many people who occasionally procrastinate are perfectly capable of handling most of the tasks they're given on a reasonable schedule. Looking at these habits of chronic procrastinators, though, can help you to overcome those moments that you do put things off. Consider carefully and honestly why you can't bring yourself to work on the task at hand. Where do you fit in Dr. Ferrari's procrastination types? Are you unsure of where to start? Do you lack confidence in your ability to complete the task required? Sometimes even just thinking about a project and why it's giving you trouble can be enough to end the procrastination. If not, there are some other things you can try to get the productive juices flowing.

1: Small tasks build toward big goals

This technique can be helpful for procrastinators of all stripes, and is especially useful when working on long and complex projects. Write down the end goal of the task that you're procrastinating at the top of a piece of paper, then start breaking it down into smaller and smaller pieces in a branching fashion until you've gotten to a level that feels manageable. Let's say, for example, that the task at hand is to put together a presentation. The second-level tasks for this project might be design a Power Point and prepare your speech. The Power Point presentation could be further divided into writing the text, preparing the graphics, making the slide transitions, and so on, until something catches your eye that you feel comfortable working on.

The main advantage of breaking down a larger task into its component parts is that it can make the entire project feel less overwhelming. It also lets you set secondary deadlines for yourself along the way, especially helpful if you know you have a tendency to put off working on larger tasks until the last minute. By sorting out the tasks, you may also find components of the project that can complement each other. In the example above, let's say you start with writing the text for your Power Point. That text can then serve as the foundation for preparing what you're going to say along with the presentation. Spotting these moments of convergence makes the entire project less daunting, while the secondary deadlines let you feel like you're accomplishing things along the way and can diminish the fear of failure in avoidance-type procrastination.

2: Prioritizing

Ordering and prioritizing the tasks at hand can be especially helpful in cases of procrastination fueled by indecision. When you have a lot on your plate, deciding what is most important or time-sensitive can help you determine which task to tackle first. Start by making a list of all the assignments, tasks, and projects you need to get done. Rank them initially from first to last in order of which you perceive to be the most important. Once you've done this, write down the deadline beside the task, along with a realistic estimate of how long it's going to take you to complete. If there's no definite deadline, assign yourself one—you're more likely to pay attention to a task that's on a ticking clock than one with a nebulous completion date. Now rank the tasks again, this time on the basis of timeliness.

The reason you want to approach this from both the deadline and the importance standpoint is that it lets you see, at a glance, where your deadlines and your priorities converge. A task that's due next week will need to get your attention now, even if you don't consider it to be so important; a task that's very important and time consuming, even though it's not due for three months, will warrant occasional attention in between other more time-sensitive assignments to prevent it from becoming a last-minute race to the end. Sketch out a rough plan of attack for all your projects, then check back to your list and revise it as you turn in projects or receive new assignments.

3: Take your project on a first date

Sometimes the hardest part of focusing on a task is knowing where to start. When this is the case, dedicating quality time to brainstorming or working on the task at hand is crucial. It's best if you can do this the analog way, using pen and paper; if your line of work demands the use of technology, turn off your Wi-Fi so you're not tempted to waste time checking your e-mail or browsing the internet. Also turn off or silence your phone and have the discipline not to check it. Unless your work demands you be in a specific office or studio space, it's best if you can go to a neutral territory that's neither in your home or your office. A coffee shop or restaurant can be perfect for this, or a public park or garden if the weather allows it. The purpose of this is two-fold. One, the change of scenery breaks you out of your normal routines and may let you approach the issue from a different angle. Two, it prevents your colleagues or family from inadvertently breaking your focus. It can also give the process an inherent reward. Let yourself get that salted caramel mocha you've been craving, or go to that little bistro you've been meaning to visit, if it will give you the motivation you need to sit down and hash out the work you've been avoiding. If you are especially sensitive to background noise, you can bring a pair of headphones and listen to music as you work; you may find, however, that the background volume in your average cafe or park is just enough white noise to let you concentrate in peace.

Give your project at least an hour; two or three is better, if you have the time for it. Treat the project like it's an attractive person, or an old friend—someone you would look forward to sharing time with. Schedule this brainstorming session in your planner and don't let yourself cancel the date unless there's an actual emergency. If you do have to cancel it, reschedule the date immediately. Don't have any expectations in mind in terms of tangible results or accomplishments. Especially if your procrastination is fueled by anxiety or a fear of failure, a preconceived expectation of results will likely only serve to make you tense up and freeze. The goal is to remove yourself from your typical constraints, letting your mind feel out the project without stress or distraction.

4: Hold yourself accountable

You often hear about people who were straight-A students through school that have trouble adjusting to the working world. There are of course a multitude of things that can cause this, but one main thing is that, in school, there is a teacher assigning tasks, setting due dates, and giving out grades to tell you how well you've done. While a performance review is something like a grade, figuring out what tasks to do and when can often be at your discretion in the workplace. If you're writing a report in a college class, you'll have separate due dates for the outline, the first draft, and so on, all the way through to the finished project. In a workplace environment, you're expected to manage your own time through the process; most people outside of school care only about your results.

If you find you're having trouble starting and finishing tasks on time, buy a notebook and designate it your work journal. Start each day writing down what you plan to accomplish, then jot down brief notes as you go through your day—when you start tasks, when you finish them, and any particular challenges or issues that arose as you were working. Review your work journal once a week. What percentage of your "to-do list" have you been accomplishing in the average day? Which tasks are taking longer than others? Are there any consistent issues that came up during your work? Workshop and review your process as if it were completed by a student, and you are the teacher. If this were a stranger's work journal, what critiques would you make of it?

A work journal lets you see which tasks you've been avoiding before they fall completely off your radar. It also lets you evaluate your work process and make the most efficient use of your day. If you're working steadily and still consistently not completing your tasks, you may be overestimating what is a realistic amount of work to accomplish in a day; that, more than procrastination, could be the source of your stress and missed deadlines.

Chapter 23: Discipline Your Rewards

It's very easy to over-compensate when you do something great. You feel that you can reward yourself. You may even stay in bed one morning because you achieved so much the previous day, but the problem with this kind of reward is that you are going backwards instead of forwards. What you need to do is discipline yourself to a reward system that actually backs up all the work that you have put in so far. Thus, make the rewards something that is appropriate to your achievements.

If you exercise each day of the week, take the weekend off, but do so with the mindset that training starts again on Monday. If you have cleared your desk, don't get lethargic. Use a reward that really does help you. Offer to help someone else with their workload and one of the biggest rewards that a human being can get from life is obtained by becoming a giving person. This only works if you can give without adding strings. For example, if you have done something great in the office, don't blow your own trumpet. Learn to be humble and pass some of your knowledge to someone else instead. Don't expect any praise for the act. You are doing this for the good of everyone and when you do things voluntarily, you get the biggest buzz you possible can get from life. The reward for overcoming your laziness is that it makes you a much better person.

When you start to create lists of things you want to do, of course, you should treat yourself to something as a celebration of what you have done, but don't get smug. People who don't procrastinate do these things every day of their lives. However, a small reward to yourself when you see all of the items ticked off on your list can go a long way to encouraging you toward doing the same thing the next day and the next day.

The problem with leaving everything at the last moment is that it robs you of the opportunity to actually enjoy your life. You are always fretting about the jobs you haven't done and changing your habits literally liberates you and gives you time for fun. Have that fun and if there are people you can enjoy that fun with, then that's a really good situation to be in. Perhaps you wanted golf club membership but were too lazy to do anything about it. Make a point of seeing to it that the rewards you give yourself are healthy and that they add something positive to your lifestyle. Make them appropriate. For example, if you have been putting off dieting for a while, an appropriate prize would not be a cream cake! It would be a much more productive prize to actually go to the stores and buy yourself something in your new size.

When you add some kind of positive reward scheme to your life, you make your life better, but if you make that reward commensurate with the tasks that you have managed to perform, that adds an element of enjoyment to achievement. For example, if you painted the back porch, how about treating yourself to that plant you always wanted but never really had space for. It will make the porch look great and show off all your hard work.

The problem with people who procrastinate is that they don't really know that rewarding feeling of achievement and most of the things that they eventually get around to doing are done in a mediocre fashion. Throughout this book, all of the calls to action have been about discipline and that means self-discipline. You have to recognize that the only person who stands in the way of your success in life is you.

Call to Action from This Chapter

Discipline yourself to finding suitable rewards for your hard work

Tick off all the jobs on your list as you finish them

If you finish them within the timeframe, you have given yourself, reward yourself

Make your rewards fit the level of achievement

Share your knowledge with others and enjoy the reward of giving

I added this chapter because giving yourself a suitable reward actually takes discipline. I remember people who I have worked with who rewarded themselves with gifts that didn't reinforce their new habits and that's bad news. It's almost like allowing yourself a cigarette because you managed to give up smoking! Discipline is the only way forward and when you discipline yourself toward achievement, you find that it's a wonderful reward on its own and that the reward you place upon that task is only a token. It's what you feel inside when you achieve that is the real gift.

Chapter 24: View Things From Different Perspectives

This is very similar to how people look at problems and finding possible solutions. One problem could have a different solution if a different approach is done. There are ways on how you can set your mind into gaining new perspective about a problem.

Get visual materials –You can produce visuals about a certain problem to see a common thing among them. This will help you see a pattern and you will be able to remember important points better.

Use a better language – When describing a problem, the language you use in describing can create a different impact on the people you are talking to and be able to shift ideas. Projects can be viewed at different angles on how to make it work.

Think of different questions – If you keep on asking the same pattern of questions, you will get the same answers and you will just go back to where you started making no room for progress. Changing your questions into something better will lead to different answers that will help you even more.

Change the way you present things — When you change things up a little bit, it will open a path of new thinking and you will be able to identify the most significant points in the issue. Not everyone will understand what you are driving at, but discussing it in a way that everybody can understand will help them give a better input. The people you talk to might even have a better way to solve it.

Have a new analysis — There are so many ways in showing a problem. If you keep on getting the same answer and perspective, do some changes. Have a different way of writing it down or visualizing it. You will be able to draw more strategies on how you can solve a particular problem.

See the bigger picture —This can improve the way you see the problem. See how it goes with the whole thing and this can improve how you have been seeing the whole thing all along. It can lead to better solutions, perspectives, and ideas. This can also help you find what you have been doing wrong which has been the reason why you are not progressing.

Collaborating and discussing a specific issue is something that makes room for progress in order to solve a problem. If you only listen to your own ideas and not have an opportunity to see it from a different angle, then you will not find other ways. Seeking other possible perspectives helps you gain more insight which can help you go through any challenge in life.

Chapter 25: Take A Nap

Taking a short, quick nap is one of the best ways to rejuvenate your body. When you take some time to pause and take a nap, you are relaxing your body from its tense position and allowing your brain to rejuvenate itself. When you come back from your slumber, you may find that you are more alert and more willing to get your work done.

When you take a nap, try taking a nap on a place other than your bed. Since your bed is so comfortable, soft, and warm, your body may mistakenly think that you are trying to go to sleep. When that happens, you may end up sleeping beyond your desired time (and worse – miss your deadline!). Try sleeping on the couch, on a chair, on the floor, or even in your car (if it's not too hot or too cold). You can basically sleep anywhere that it's safe and not worry too much about going to sleep.

To rectify the issue of oversleeping, you can set your alarm for a target time to wake up. A good amount of time to nap for is one hour, but each person is different. You may find that 30 minutes is enough for you, or even 15 minutes of shut eye is enough to completely renew yourself. To find this effective time, you will have to experiment until you find the best napping period for you.

When you awaken from your nap, make sure to take a deep breath, yawn, and stretch out your arms into the air! What this does is it tells your body and subsconscious that it's time to get up. Then, quickly jump onto your feet with a quick burst of energy and tell yourself that you will get that work done!

Lastly, make sure that you don't tempt yourself to get back into a second nap. This works best if you do not look at your napping area at all, and also if you clean up the area after your slumber. This means that you should fold any blankets and remove any pillows in the area. Trust me, napping gets really addictive, and I was at one point unable to function with my daily nap! Naps are meant to help boost your productivity, not hinder it!

Side Note: In hispanic speaking countries, citizens are often allowed to take breaks from their normal work day. The people would often go home, take a bite to eat, and nap during this time. They call this a "Siesta", and it is a welcome tradition to their cultures.

Chapter 26: Bathroom Hacks

Simple Methods to Clean The Toilet And Bathroom

You can tell about a person's overall hygiene by taking one glance at their bathroom. Whether you have a big house or a cozy, small house, the bathroom tends to get dirty more often than all the other rooms.

The bathroom is prone to infestation of germs and this is all the more reason why it should be cleaned often and with much care. Most homeowners will attest to the fact that when it comes to cleaning the bathroom, you cannot do it in the shortest time you wish.

Note that, in order to have a sparkling bathroom, you do not have to spend hours scrubbing it. All you need is a general maintenance routine that will ensure that your bathroom stays germ-free and clean at all times.

For instance, you can make it a routine to always wipe the bathtub and the glass door (s) with a non-fluffy towel each time you are done bathing. This helps you to counter the grime that tends to build up.

This will take less than 3 minutes of your time and yet give you satisfactory results. Ensure that you have a few non-fluffy washcloths on standby, together with detergent in a spray bottle. Once you are done with your ablutions, spray the sink and the toilet seat with the solution and water, then wipe off.

While at it, disinfect the doorknobs and clean them with another cloth. This is a sure way of keeping germs and viruses at bay. Lastly, squirt some bathroom detergent on the floor and wipe it with a rag. In a record 10 minutes, you will have a germ-free bathroom.

Have a Clean Bathroom using Home Remedy Tips

Contrary to popular belief, you do not have to spend much on bathroom detergents in order to have a clean bathroom. You will be pleasantly surprised to learn that, by following a few home remedy tips, you can achieve excellent results as far as your bathroom is concerned. These remedies are also known as green cleaning tips and here are a few of them:

Baking Soda

Baking soda is the mother of all remedies and, when it comes to the bathroom, it works marvelously, especially in countering bad odors. Sprinkle a generous amount on the sink drain, allow it to sit for a couple of minutes and then rinse it off.

If the odor is too strong, you could combine baking soda with white vinegar, allow the concoction to sit for half an hour and rinse with cold water. This will leave your bathroom looking fresh and clean.

Lemon

If you notice stains and grime in your bathroom, then it is time to employ the reliable power of the lemon. Rub a fresh slice of lemon over a stain, allow it to sit for a while and then wipe it off with a damp cloth. The stain or grime will be gone.

Vinegar

Since time immemorial, vinegar has been used and revered as the best and most effective bathroom cleaner. Vinegar has many uses around the house and it is cost effective as compared to most detergents on the market.

Use vinegar to clean off grime, doorknobs, the sink and the drainage. It clears off those stubborn rings that tend to sit in the toilet bowl. Leave it overnight and scrub it off in the morning. If you are dealing with a stainless steel sink, soak a non-fluffy cloth in vinegar and dab the cloth with a drop of oil, use the cloth to wipe the sink and the bowl and there you will have a sparkling clean sink.

Coke and Stains

The stain that forms around the rim of toilet water is always an eyesore. Different cleaners will remove a bit of the stain, but Coke will remove the stain easily.

Many will find it hard to empty a bottle of Coke down the toilet but it is the only way to remove the difficult stains in your toilet.

Pour it around the rim of the toilet and let it settle for about an hour.

The chemicals and enzymes in the coke will help to kill the germs and remove the ugly stain. The slight stain that will be left can easily be removed with the toilet brush. Flush your toilet after you are through and there you will have yourself a sparkling clean toilet.

Other drinks that will help clean your bathroom are vodka and alcohol. They help remove mildew on the bathroom caulk. Bathroom grout can also be cleaned by making a paste of baking soda and water and smearing it on the grout.

When you add a water and vinegar solution, the paste will foam and you can then rinse everything. The paste will remove the dirt from the grout and you will have a clean bathroom again

Treat the Bathroom with Baby Oil

Keep your bathroom porcelain shiny by applying some drops of baby oil, and then dab with a soft cloth. You can also use this method to shine the sink and toilet areas.

Note: Always steer clear of pungent air freshener sprays, as they are harmful. Instead, use cinnamon sticks or potpourri. Alternatively, you could dab a little body spray on the bathroom bulb. This will give your bathroom a lasting scent once you switch on the lights.

Chapter 27: Habits Related To Wealth And Productivity

The following headings are habits that are very important in any quest for wealth and increased productivity.

Use your daily Checklist

The first habit you were told to perform in this book was to make a daily checklist of tasks that have been prioritized. This habit is crucially important and if you really want to succeed cannot be stressed enough. If you do not make a daily checklist then it becomes much harder to acquire the habit of practicing self-control.

Don't Waste Time

- This is a no brainer.
- Time is like land; there is only a limited supply of it.
- Time is irreplaceable and once it has gone then it is gone forever.
- Much of the demands on our time are rubbish.

- Many hours are spent every year in the doing of things that we would probably be better not doing.
- What is an hour of your time really worth?
- We are here to achieve and not just to do.
- Make sure that you do the right thing and not just absorb yourself in doing things right.
- Don't hesitate in abandoning habits and rituals such as checking social media.

Pay Off Debt

This needs to be a habit and NOT an optional extra.

- Sadly when some people get into debt they take on more debt in order to pay off the previous debt and as they do so they fall deeper into debt. They reduce their credit score.
- If you pay off your debt then it is a much better option than investing as you do not pay any taxes on debts that you pay off

whereas you usually have to pay taxes on interest that you get from investments

- If you pay off debts then you reduce stress.
- Once an asset is paid off then any increase in value becomes yours and this is particularly so in the case of real estate.
- If you do not pay off your debts then you have to deal with people who lend money and these are often very unpleasant people. They are in the business of making money and not making friends.

Count the Cost

Many people fail to do this and end up paying a lot in the long run. They are often the sorts of people who wonder where the money goes. If you are one of them then you need to acquire the habit of counting the cost. This also applies to someone in business. Business costs must be tracked otherwise serious damage can be done to your enterprise.

Here is a very simple example. Supermarkets often put confectionery near the checkout. The harassed shopper sees a delicious Hershey bar for a $1 and decides to buy it. They go shopping at the supermarket three days a week. They buy three bars each week. There are fifty-two weeks in a year. They are on holiday for two weeks so they buy the three bars fifty times. Over a year that is $150!! Ouch!

Be Positive

If at work you are an unhappy or angry person you will lower the outlook and morale of many of your colleagues. You may even threaten their health, particularly if you are the boss. Everyone wants to collaborate with happy, optimistic, positive and cheerful people; few wish to be around or have to endure those who are angry, sullen or moody.

Learn a new skill

Sometimes this is vital and, if you don't, your very job may disappear. This is happening with ever-greater frequency. Many are the young person who was told in the 1970s that learning to use a typewriter was a passport to job security. This advice was not accurate. Modern offices seem to be bereft of typewriters. Indeed the only place you can be sure of finding one now is in a museum!

The learning of new skills will make you more useful and employable. Be careful in learning new skills that you do so in a way, which helps your goals.

Suppose you were keen to learn a new computer language called Kax. Let's use the support habits listed in Chapter 4.

You must be able to concentrate attention on Kax.

As far as possible forget time while learning Kax. It is what you put into the time you're learning in not the time itself that is important.

Dispense with thoughts of the past without Kax or the future with it.

Study Kax when you are both relaxed and alert. When you do so put aside concerns that are not related to the task of learning Kax.

You can see the application of the supporting habits for the learning of Kax.

The learning of new skills is particularly important if you embrace the next habit.

Apply for new jobs

This is not a good habit to have if you are completely happy with your current position. However, sometimes the current position has become impossible and you must move on. In such a case you should acquire a habit stack of applying for new jobs.

Never invest more than you can afford to lose

This should be well known, however, it is best illustrated with an example. Few have not heard of Bitcoin and other cryptocurrencies. Should you buy cryptocurrency as soon as you can? Some experts say so, with some believing that its value will keep rising, with one Bitcoin valued at $100,000 inside a decade. Cryptocurrencies may appear odd now, but it is sensible to recall that when Apple, Microsoft, and other technology companies began moving forward during the 1980s, there were people who thought personal computers had no future. History has proved these people were wrong and people who were astute enough to buy shares in Apple or Microsoft are financially very happy now.

Despite this, you must always exercise care and caution, the rise in the price of an asset does not mean that its true worth is increasing. There are many good examples of this throughout the history of investment, with a very unfortunate one being the U.S. real estate boom of the late 2000s. Sometimes prices are driven up by hype and outright lies. It is always sensible to remember that if something ascends it usually descends.

Spread your investments

Within any investment portfolio you have, you should have different investments, there are many to select from. This process goes by the name of, 'spreading the risk', do not forget the saying that you should not put all your eggs in only one basket.

Chapter Summary

- Acquire these habits.
- Use your daily checklist.
- Don't waste time.
- Pay off debt.
- Count the cost.
- Be positive
- Learn a new skill.
- Possibly apply for a new job.
- Never invest more than you can afford to lose.
- Spread your assets.

Chapter 28: Upgrade Your Key Skills

One way to stop the habit of procrastination is to reassess your soft skills. Unlike hard skills, which are the skills that are typically learned in a classroom and are easy to quantify, soft skills are more like personality traits. It is easy to become a bit lax in your habits when nobody else is relying on you. Unfortunately, those habits contribute to your personality traits. When you get too comfortable at a job or even in your personal life, your soft skills may need a bit of an upgrade. If you want to stop procrastinating, try taking a look at your key skills and ask yourself if they could be improved. It may be difficult to admit that you need help in these areas, but it will pay off in the end.

Communication

Effective communication isn't just about the way you communicate. It also refers to when you communicate. If you know you have to have an uncomfortable conversation with someone, or if you simply don't like talking to people, it is easy to tell yourself, "I'll do it later." But when it is a conversation that could affect the other person, it can be harmful to wait until later, both for the other person and for yourself. For example, consider needing a favor from someone and then finding out that person can't accommodate you in such a short time frame. That's your loss. Or you need to plan a meeting with work and keep rescheduling. That's showing that you're inconsiderate of other people's time. If you don't want to be seen that way, start sticking to your commitments and get those conversations over within a timely manner.

Team Player

Someone who is a team player typically respects the opinions of their team members, as well as their time. They communicate regularly and stay on top of their tasks to help the entire team achieve their goals. You can see how procrastination can affect an entire team when there is one person who fails to pull their weight because they waited too long.

Think back to any task that either required cooperation from other people or required you to meet a goal that other people were relying on. Did your lack of time management affect them in any way? If so, try to change your habits so people can consider you to be a real team player. There are tips later in this book.

Project Management

Managing a project and having other people rely on you for that project means that you have to kick those procrastination habits to the curb. Although a project manager typically leads a team instead of doing the work themselves, project management also includes delegating, monitoring progress, and effectively communicating. They're looking at you as a leader, so it is important that you set them up for success by organizing, planning and supporting them. To do that, you need to manage your time like a professional. Project management is a very important soft skill to master, especially in the workplace.

Chapter 29: Rules To Get You Started With Your To-Do List

Aside from the partitioning of your to-do list into sections, there are other rules you need to consider to keep your to-do list well managed.

Without utilizing these rules, you might end up falling for issues that make other lists fail.

Do not overload your list

This rule deals with the maximum activities on your to-do list should contain in each section.

One of the many causes of a failed to-do list especially those automated ones (smartphones and computers) is that the list may get too long and overwhelming.

We usually find it difficult to resist adding an activity to the to-do list. Worst still, it becomes more difficult erasing the tasks as we feel they are more important or urgent.

Ensure that your to-do list (especially the high priority section) is restricted to only activities that have immediate due dates.

Do not overload it either. Pick tasks that you are sure you can complete within a stipulated time.

You cannot eat more than you can chew.

Your high priority section should be five items or less short

Your to-do list can only be effective if it contains as few tasks as possible.

Five would be reasonable.

If you include more than five tasks, you may not complete them in due time and may forget undertaking some.

So, how do can you manage to maintain five or fewer tasks in your high priority section? It is quite easy.

Before adding a task to this section, you can always ask yourself if you have the time to complete the work past the normal time. If you feel you can't, it is appropriate to leave the task. Do not strain on it; you may end up being unresourceful and unreliable.

This strict rule ensures your to-do list is well controlled and you finish the tasks on time.

So when coming up with a to-do list, especially the high priority section, always ensure it is under five items.

Your medium priority section should have ten or fewer items

This rule applies to the medium priority section of your to-do list.

Remember your to-do list contains those activities that you plan to do, during the day, or after that day. Therefore they are not urgent. Since these items are not extremely urgent, the section tends to contain more activities making it bigger.

It becomes bigger because you tend to add more items before you complete the ones already on the list.

To manage the tasks in this section, there is a certain rule you need to consider. Keep the list under ten items.

You may wonder why to keep your list at ten or below. Well, ten items are the maximum you can easily go through and understand in one glance at the list.

You need to properly understand this list since it is a list that you check when you have some time available (when not working on urgent tasks).

Also, items in this section are those that might be coming soon, in the evening maybe, and you want to keep track of them. If you fail to check up on them, you might fail to work on them leading to failure in place of work.

That is why it is essential that you keep the list of tasks at ten or below.

It is also advisable that you regularly check on your to-do list at certain intervals depending on the sections. You could for instance check after 30 minutes or one hour for the high priority section, half a day for the medium priority section and may be daily on the low priority section.

It allows you to minimize the amount of time you spend on your to-do list limiting you to only what is needed at the current time.

Chapter 30: Reframing Failure Failure And Procrastination

Failure, the one obstacle that everyone is guaranteed to face at least several times in life. An inevitable outcome that, no matter how hard we try, can't always be avoided.

But if failure is inevitable, why do people still fear it?

Some are afraid of failure because they were constantly told that winning is the only option, so they haven't had the chance to accommodate the idea of losing; others think that failure is a sign of weakness and maladjustment.

No matter how you choose to put it, failure has and will always have an unpleasant component that makes it difficult for people to adjust to it. Although the ideal option would be to avoid failure, there are circumstances in which winning is just impossible. Maybe things didn't go according to plan, maybe something unexpected occurred. Who knows?

Sometimes, we sabotage ourselves by focusing on failure more than we should. Just like we discussed in Chapter 2 (Why do we procrastinate?), procrastination provides an escape route that allows us to avoid failure. Unfortunately, this flawed strategy is merely an illusion, because the more we delay a particular task, the higher our chance of failing.

Maybe there's another way to interpret failure...

The benefits of failing

As strange as it may sound, failure can sometimes be beneficial to our mental, emotional and spiritual growth. Once we understand the benefits of failure, we will no longer be afraid of it. In other words, instead of perceiving it as something completely out of the ordinary, we can transform it into a highly useful tool.

Here's how failure can enrich your experience:

Failure makes you stronger. Anyone trying to fulfill a dream or accomplish a goal should consider the possibility of failing. No doubt there will be plenty of criticism, setbacks and obstacles along the way, and you can't let yourself be discouraged every time you encounter such unpleasant events. But every roadblock you surpass, all the nasty criticism you endure, and every disappointment you face, will make you stronger. At some point, not only will you tolerate failure, but you will welcome it as a chance to increase resilience.

Failure exposes your soft spots. When something doesn't go as planned, most people tend to get extremely frustrated and disappointed, and as a result, they end up procrastinating. You can choose to follow the same destructive path or you can use this opportunity to become more aware of your flaws. No one is or will ever be perfect. People fall into the category of 'work in progress.' More specifically, the whole process of personal growth is a cycle of repairs, adjustments, and improvements. In this context, failure can act as a diagnostic tool, revealing the 'cracks' that need urgent fixing.

Failure gives you a reality check. Although normal life is sprinkled with both accomplishments and failures, some people insist on focusing exclusively on the brighter side of things. While this approach is praiseworthy, let's not forget that failure still exists, whether we choose to see it or not. By being aware of the failures that life occasionally 'blesses' you with, you can adopt a realistic worldview that will keep you safe from unrealistic expectations and standards.

Will failure be an extreme event and a reason to postpone your tasks, or a great opportunity to test your limits and work on your skills? The choice is yours.

There's no success without failure

How many failures are you prepared to endure to reach your goals? Pause for a moment to contemplate this question.

Take a closer look at the world's most famous entrepreneurs, athletes, scientists and artists. Do you think they were successful from day one? Do you think each and every one of their decisions was the right one? You think they've never tasted the bitterness of defeat?

The truth is, they've all failed more than a couple of times in their life and so will you. There's no reason to procrastinate and delay the start of a project, just because you might fail at some point. No amount of planning, worrying and double-checking will ever guarantee success, so you best get used to the idea that failure might occasionally mess with your day-to-day activities. Procrastination won't help either because delaying a task or project will only make things worse.

Success comes after failure which means that failure is the road to success.

Conclusion

There are lots of ways to overcome procrastination, and to get you moving into the desired directions. People who procrastinate often feel stuck and enslaved by their procrastination. The truth is, everything in life is in constant motion. You can decide to change at any moment. You can make the conscious choice not to see yourself as stuck anymore and become more aligned with the "universal laws". You'll find that, when you do, life becomes a whole lot easier, and much more fun!

Take a moment to select a tip from this book that fits your lifestyle, tackle one main procrastinated project and lift the burden from your life today!

If you enjoyed this book, please leave a review! I would love to hear your feedback!

CPSIA information can be obtained
at www.ICGtesting.com
Printed in the USA
LVHW021146090720
660099LV00007B/335

9 781989 920985